UNDERSTANDING YOUR
Child's Dreams

UNDERSTANDING YOUR
Child's Dreams

PAM SPURR PhD

ILLUSTRATIONS BY CAROLINE UFF

Sterling Publishing Co., Inc.
New York

This book is dedicated to my children, Sam and Stephie – live your dreams;
to my parents Art and Winnie – for encouraging me to live mine;
and my husband Nick – you are a dream come true.

AN EDDISON•SADD EDITION
Edited, designed and produced by
Eddison Sadd Editions Limited
St Chad's House
148 King's Cross Road
London WC1X 9DH

Library of Congress
Cataloguing-in-Publication Data Available

10 9 8 7 6 5 4 3 2 1

Published in 1999 by Sterling Publishing Company, Inc.
387 Park Avenue South, New York, N.Y. 10016

Distributed in Canada by Sterling Publishing
c/o Canadian Manda Group, One Atlantic Avenue, Suite 105
Toronto, Ontario, Canada M6K 3E7

Phototypeset in Bembo and Futura using QuarkXPress on Apple Macintosh
Origination by Atlas Mediacom (S) Pte Ltd, Singapore
Printed in Hong Kong

Sterling ISBN 0-8069-1913-2

Contents

Foreword

It is an honor to be asked to write a foreword to Dr. Pam Spurr's new book, *Understanding Your Child's Dreams*. All people dream, and children are especially active and vivid dreamers. Our dreams allow us to more safely explore our aspirations, fantasies, and also fears of daily life in the haven of our beds and freedom of our unconscious minds. Dreams are quite varied in content and form as our unconscious mind is not fettered by the conventions of everyday life and is free to make associations as it pleases. Dreams may reflect the dreamer's recent or long-past experiences quite accurately or may obscure them in fantastic symbolism.

Children often regard their dreams as a happy playground which they enter as they fall off to sleep, and they are often eager to relate their wonderful dream experiences to adults who will listen. They are invariably thrilled when their parents take a genuine interest in their dreamtime exploits. On the occasions that children experience nightmares, they look to their parents for reassurance that their terrifying phantasms are not real and, with the right approach, these nightmares can be banished from their sleeptimes.

In this book, Dr. Spurr gives parents many insights into the dreams children have. She particularly emphasizes the significance that the objects and symbols contained in children's dreams have regarding a child's relationship with his or her parents, peers, and school. In other words, Dr. Spurr gives parents a guide to understanding some of the most fundamental relationships a child may have and dream about. By seeking to understand their child's dreams, parents will surely open up a wonderful opportunity for closeness and warmth with their child that they may otherwise not fully develop or may even miss. They may also develop an understanding of some of the difficulties and conflicts their child may be experiencing in their life at home and at school before these problems spiral out of control through neglect.

Dr. Spurr divides her book into easily read and applied sections which introduce and delineate the three basics types of dreams - reality-based dreams, fantastic dreams, and nightmares - and practical approaches to understanding them. She also discusses the important principles of nurturing children's personal development through stimulation of their interests, responsiveness and positiveness to their thoughts and behavior and, most importantly, valuing your child for who they are and showing them warmth.

Dr. Spurr guides the understanding of your child's dreams with her Dream Key, which emphasizes appreciating the 1) details of your child's dreams, 2) recognition by your child of persons, places, and feelings in dreams, 3) emotions experienced during dreaming, 4) actions by or to your child in dreams, and 5) meaning attached by your child to his or her dream. She further facilitates the sharing and interpreting of your child's dreams with her Dreamercises, which are designed to allow your child to elaborate on the dreams, and the Dream Directory, which details interpretations of commonly experienced dream themes.

Dr. Spurr relates the actual case examples of the dreams of twenty-four children and how the dreams related to the real-life experiences of the children involved. She details what actions the parents took to help their children with both the positive and negative signifigances of their dreams. In "A Garden Full of Wonder," Sophie, a four year old, dreams of a beautiful garden of flowers and fantastic bees. In relating her dream to her mother, Susan, Sophie communicates her curiosity about the rapidly expanding world around her. Susan, who was beginning to become somewhat frustrated with all of Sophie's "Why?"s, is re-invigorated in her desire to remain responsive to Sophie's many questions as

she thinks about the meanings for the dream. This dream and the other case histories show parents the many ways they can create a greater and enduring closeness with their children by listening to and sharing in their children's dreams.

It is also a pleasure to write this foreword as Dr. Spurr is also my sister Pam and I believe our work has many parallels. She is, of course, a Ph.D. Psychologist and I, on the other hand, am an M.D. emergency medicine specialist with an additional background in sociology and social psychology. Pam's goal is to give parents a greater understanding of, and warmth and closeness to, their children - that is, to heal their relationships, while I am trying to heal their bodies. In the E.R., I see great contrasts in the closeness and warmth between parents and their children. Many families that I care for in the E.R. are clearly very closely knit and affectionate. However, all too often I find parents and their children sadly disconnected and in both physical and emotional distress. Of course the E.R. is not exactly where people come to be happy per se, but I do believe that my patients do much better when they have close and affectionate family ties. I also believe that warmth and closeness are fostered by sharing dreams . . . the essence of my sister's book.

Douglas Spurr, M.D., M.A.

Introduction

Parents usually look surprised when I mention my interest in children's dreams. They remark: *'I've never thought about that – I guess children do dream!'* And their interest is immediately ignited. This is usually quickly followed by concern that for some time they have been missing out on part of the rich tapestry of their child's inner world. At this point I always reassure them that it is never too late to learn how to tap into their child's marvellous dreamworld.

Children are prolific dreamers. They are less inhibited than adults and less concerned about concealing anything unpleasant in their dreams. When adults dream of something that makes them feel uncomfortable, they frequently dismiss the dream on waking, frightened to acknowledge their discomfort and the possible causes of it in their waking life. Although children are in the process of developing such subconscious protective mechanisms, they are much more likely to be eager to share their dream experiences with their parents. On the other hand, they may have difficulty communicating their dream experiences through lack of understanding of particular images or the emotions aroused by them or through insufficient vocabulary to describe their dreams adequately. Or they may simply feel that you are too busy to spend time listening to them as they recount their dreams to you.

This book shows you how to open up communication with your child, so that they find it easier to talk to you about their dreams. In doing so, you will undoubtedly discover an inspiring source of creativity and joy, or, alternatively, signposts to the kinds of problems they are encountering in waking life. And you will foster a closer, warmer relationship with your child, which is bound to bring you both pleasure and be beneficial to your child's personal development.

Dreams and Child Development

Your child's emotional, social and intellectual, or cognitive, development is an extremely complex process that begins in the womb. There, the developing baby is affected by far more than their mother's diet. It is now acknowledged that the mother's entire lifestyle plays a part in the development of their unborn baby. Everything from the music she listens to and the amount of conversation and social interaction she takes part in, to her moods and level of physical activity, all make their mark on the unborn baby, who is already able to dream!

Your child's emotional, social and cognitive development – which together comprise their personality – are inextricably linked. For example, a child deprived of warmth and affection will be less able to relate to other children, so affecting their social development. They may also find it hard to express emotion, or express it inappropriately, perhaps exhibiting aggressive outbursts, so their emotional development will also be affected. Poor social and emotional development may in turn lead to loss of interest in intellectually stimulating tasks, so affecting their cognitive development.

Your child's dreams mirror the state of their developing personality. If they are developing emotionally, socially and cognitively without any problems then their dreams will be full of happy and creative events and feelings. If their dreams contain disturbing images or emotions, then it may be that they are encountering some sort of problem in their personal development. Careful exploration of the dream can help you determine which aspect is causing them problems.

The River of Personality

Think of your child's personality as a flowing river. A river bends and changes in character as it moves further and further away from its source, while retaining its own core unique identifiable qualities.

The water in the river may be likened to the emotional element of your child's personality – turbulent and gentle by turns, depending on what lies in its path. It churns angrily as it encounters obstacles, gushes excitedly down steeper inclines and flows serenely down gentle slopes.

The banks represent your child's social development. They contain the emotional waters, providing buffers when the flow becomes over-excited, and they adapt in size and shape as the waters expand and mature. Without the banks, or social development, your child would be unable to form friendships and adapt to the demands of their social environment. Of course, a turbulent river can overwhelm the banks, jeopardizing your child's social activities, but this occurs less as they realize the negative social effects of their badly managed emotions.

Finally, there are the many and varied contents of the river, which represent your child's cognitive development. The rocks, pebbles, and plant and animal life may be likened to the skills and problem-solving abilities that grow in number and complexity as a child matures. If the emotional waters of the river dry up, so too will the developing cognitive skills.

Nurturing your Child's Personal Development

Exploring your child's dreams with them is one of the ways in which you can help nurture the development of your child's personality, so that it becomes a robust river capable of accommodating all the many bends, obstacles, floods and droughts of life. There are five basic principles to bear in mind when trying to encourage strong emotional, social and cognitive development in your child.

The first principle is stimulation: an understimulated child will not thrive and develop. Cuddle, talk to and play with your child; introduce them to music and teach them about the world. The more varied the stimulation, the broader their range of experience. And as your child experiences more of what the world has to offer, so they will want to carry on exploring that world. Stimulation is the key factor in maintaining momentum for their ongoing cognitive development. Exploring their dreams with them can provide the inspiration for the introduction of new or creative pursuits, such as writing or painting.

The second principle to consider is responsiveness. Demonstrate by your behavior that you are actively listening and responding to your child. This establishes what is known as 'reciprocal interaction' in which you and your child respond to each other. The more frequently you respond to their behavior, the more they will have pleasure in your company. The more pleasure they show in interacting with you, the more pleasure you will derive from interacting with them. Responding to their dreams can form a creative and unique part of this cycle.

The third principle is positiveness. This means praising the positive behavior of your child, consequently encouraging more of it. The more frequently you notice and encourage the positive actions of your child, the more likely they are to thrive and develop into an adult with a positive outlook and inner confidence. It means focusing on the positive in ordinary daily life to create a generally positive environment. By responding positively to your child's dream life you demonstrate to them that life is not just about routine and duty to others. It is also about them, their feelings, thoughts and dreams.

The fourth principle is to value your child for who they are. Happy, emotionally well-adjusted adults were invariably allowed to be themselves as children (this does not mean allowed to run wild!). They were not compared unfavorably to an older sibling or a neighbor's child. They were not used as vessels to fulfil their parents' dreams; for example, forced to take drama by a mother who always wanted to be an actress. By exploring your child's dreams you are valuing something that is uniquely theirs, giving them the message that you are interested in their hopes and ambitions, their inner life.

The final principle is warmth. Warmth does not necessarily mean that you have to be a 'touchy-feely' parent. Warmth can be conveyed by vocal tone, encouragement, being there when your child needs you, and kind, affectionate remarks. Many parents fear that showing their child warmth will develop emotional weakness in their child. The opposite is true. A child who has experienced warmth will be able to demonstrate compassion and warmth to others and will develop an inner strength. Listening to and discussing your child's dreams provides you with many opportunities to share warm moments.

Levels of Consciousness

A new-born baby does not distinguish between what is happening now and what happened yesterday. They do not think in terms of being awake or being asleep. They are cognitively, emotionally and socially extremely active, acutely interested in everything around them, particularly the smells, sounds and images related to their primary caregiver and immediate environment. However, they do not define these experiences in the same way as adults.

As your infant becomes a child they become more aware of different levels of consciousness, or awareness. They know what it means to have 'been asleep' and what it means to 'pay attention'. They are probably aware that their mother is calling them in the distance as they watch their favorite program on television, and they choose to ignore her!

Consider your child's mind as a fantastic, extremely long garden, containing one section after the other of lush plant life. Each section is connected to the next by a garden gate. As you plunge deeper into the garden, you find that the gates are closed ever more tightly to seal in memories, feelings, beliefs and attitudes. The very deepest sections of your child's lush, fertile 'garden' are 'secret', contained in the unconscious part of their mind.

This secret garden serves as a playground for your child's emotional life. Their feelings, thoughts, worries and creative energy all slip down into their unconscious where they are stored in their secret garden – their own private world. Sometimes, one of the deeper sections contains memories of unpleasant events, imprisoned by an extremely effective gate, or protective mechanism, so that they do not disturb your child during their waking life. Even so, your child's waking behavior and dream life may be directly related to some of the memories contained in the garden beyond this gate.

The nature and purpose of sleep

We spend a staggering third of our lives asleep and until recently it was thought that we did so in order to replenish energy levels and revitalize our powers of thought. Most scientists now agree that the primary function of sleep may be to allow dreaming!

Research has shown that the brain undergoes many transformations during sleep. Measured by electrical activity, these transformations are viewed as a series of stages. Stage one occurs as you fall asleep. You feel drowsy and are semi-conscious of your surroundings as you start to meander down the garden path towards the deeper reaches of your secret garden. During stages two and three you gradually fall deeper into an unconscious state. After approximately twenty to thirty minutes you fall into stage four, or 'slow-wave' sleep. This is the deepest level of sleep from which you are able to 'see' your secret garden.

After approximately ninety minutes of stage-four sleep, the pattern of your brain waves suddenly changes into what appears as a burst of activity even more lively than that recorded during waking hours. At the same time, the eye muscles jerk and twitch, giving rise to the term 'rapid eye movement' sleep, or 'REM'. The REM stage lasts for about twenty minutes and re-emerges at ninety-minute intervals.

People woken up during REM sleep report that they were dreaming. The gates of your child's secret garden have opened enough for your child to be able to 'see' the vivid imagery contained within it as they sleep.

During stage-four sleep you move about and some people even sleep walk, but during REM sleep your body undergoes 'sleep paralysis'. Your whole body is paralyzed apart from your chest, to allow you to breathe, and your eyes, which do not stop moving. Researchers believe that paralysis occurs during the dreaming phase of sleep in order to prevent you from acting out your dreams and harming yourself.

Unborn babies do not experience sleep paralysis, and scientists believe that this is because nature 'knows' the baby is completely protected in the womb. In fact, when pregnant women feel their baby moving, the baby may well be dreaming. Many scientists believe that during their dream phases the unborn baby is processing what it can hear from inside the womb. Infants scream out sometimes when asleep as though having a nightmare, and babies experience a huge amount of REM time that diminishes with age.

Gateway to the Mind's Secret Garden

So what is the purpose of dreaming? A wealth of studies has found that REM sleep deprivation results in emotional difficulties. So dreaming appears to keep you both emotionally and psychologically healthy. Most dream researchers agree that dreaming allows you to process experiences and feelings of meaning to you. The limbic system, the more primitive part of the brain, goes frantic with electrical activity during REM sleep, indicating a very real need for the deepest levels of the mind to go into free flow during its dreaming phase.

Only during stage-four sleep do the latches of the deeper garden gates of the unconscious loosen to allow some of this emotional life to slip through in the form of dreams and nightmares. If your child wakes at the right moment they may be able to recall at least part of their dream, to give an indication of what their mind has chosen to mull over. Sometimes this unlocks a natural creativity languishing within your child or shows your child how to solve a minor problem. Nightmares occur when their unconscious cannot cope with the emotional turbulence contained there. In this case, your child will wake abruptly with terrible, often apparently inexplicable-seeming, images at the forefront of their mind.

There are many benefits to taking time to explore your child's dreams with them. It will help you to communicate with each other better, improving mutual understanding and providing you with a wealth of fascinating knowledge about their beliefs and attitudes.

Although it can be difficult to disentangle the meaningful symbolism of the dream from the rest of the dream imagery, with practice and care, you can gain a feeling for the symbolism inherent in your child's dreams. With time, you will be able to discover through their dreams what excites and fascinates them at any given moment, providing you with the basis for creative projects or new activities. Equally, you may gain valuable insight into a problem your child is experiencing or the stage of development they have reached. Hopefully, sharing this time with your child will encourage their creative expression and self-confidence.

Encouraging Dream Awareness

Creating dream awareness in children is the first step to understanding their dreams together. This is a gradual process. Begin by recounting to them a dream you have had. Whatever their age, a child will find this interesting. They will wonder at the strange occurrences that went on in your mind. If they have never really been aware of dreaming before, they may be fascinated and ask you numerous questions about your dream. Fill in the details for them at the level you think they will understand.

Next, if they are very young, ask them if they have ever had a dream. If your child is older they may well have told you of their nightmares and possibly their dreams, too, but you have never thought about exploring them. If this is the situation, ask your child at breakfast one day if they dreamed the night before. Allow the new communication with your child to develop slowly.

Once your child is used to talking about their dreams and listening to you talking about yours, start to encourage them positively to dream. At bedtime talk to them about dreaming and all the wonderful possibilities that exist in dreamland. If you read them a bedtime story, suggest they might like to revisit the story in their dreams. Alternatively, ask them about the best moments of the day and suggest they revisit one of them. Children often retain vivid memories of special events or happy moments from the past. Perhaps your child would like to revisit one of these in their dreams. For further ideas, read through each of the dreamercises (*see pages 118–25*).

As they go to sleep, ask them to try to remember their dreams in the morning. Encourage them to keep paper and pencil by the bed, so that when they wake they can immediately sketch some of the images arising from the dream or write a few words about it. This could become their special 'dream book'. You might like to photocopy the Dream Diary pages provided in this book (*see pages 126–29*) for this purpose.

The Three Types of Dream

In general, dreams tend to fall into one of the following three categories: reality-based, positive development dreams; creative and fantastic dreams; and nightmares and dreams with disturbing qualities.

• **Reality-based Dreams** usually reflect a positive aspect of your child's experience of life, or reveal that they have reached a particular developmental stage. Such dreams center around a recognizable past or present event, situation or relationship and may be positively exciting or more ordinary in feeling. Reality-based dreams range from the extremely detailed 'recollective' dream, in which actual events are replayed, to the dream in which the story is entirely a creation of the child's imagination but the people, place and situation is realistic.

Reality-based dreams can tell you a great deal about which experiences have made the most impact on your child, and can illuminate the nature of a particular relationship or indicate how their interests and personality are developing. Juan's dream (*see page 26*) reveals just how a routine visit to the local museum fired his interest in a whole new subject.

The occasional inclusion of an unrelated detail can provide insight into the way your child links life events with something else of meaning to them. In Jane's dream (*see page 74*), the difficulties she is having in accepting the new woman in her widowed father's life are transferred to her favorite party dress, which has changed so that she no longer likes it.

• **Fantastic Dreams** can provide you with a wealth of material about your child's developing self. The fantastic adventures and outrageous dreamscapes they create may simply be the product of your child's growing creativity or each may contain a deeper, symbolic meaning. If this is the case, you can seize the moment and facilitate your child's new interest or developing skill.

In Antonio's dream (*see page 50*), he pilots a super spacecraft in a great adventurous dreamscape. Although fantastic, his dream represents his adventurous self and his parents are able to build on his enthusiasms. Use fantastic dreams to further creativity through the media of arts and crafts, story-writing and drama.

• **Nightmares** are overtly terrifying and cause children a great deal of anxiety, while any dreams that contain disturbing qualities are extremely unpleasant. Experiencing either indicates that your child has met with a specific or generalized problem. Some nightmares relate to a single discreet event, such as being scolded by a teacher.

Many children experience problems that they are simply unable to describe; others try to bury problems that make them feel uncomfortable beneath the day-to-day routine, unable to decide what to do about them or even to face them square on. So the strange imagery that sometimes occurs in a nightmare often serves to protect the child from facing the origins of their discomfort. Their subconscious throws a veil over the real issue even if it cannot quite prevent a nightmare from occurring because of it.

Sensitive handling of nightmares is important. In addition to reassuring your child, it is important to understand and deal with the cause of the nightmare by developing good, effective communication with your child, and to discharge the 'power' of the nightmare by using an appropriate dreamercise (*see pages 123–25*).

Exploring your Child's Dreams

A dream may arise from something your child was doing shortly before bedtime or earlier in day. Alternatively, it may symbolize your child's feelings towards an ongoing issue that they are wrestling with at deeper levels of their consciousness. Or it may evolve out of a memory that holds special meaning for them. Some dreams fall between positive development dreams and fantastical ones. Some dreams are purely entertaining. If you cannot discover how your child's dream is linked to their life, feelings or activities, treat it as a creative springboard for your child. Do not struggle to find meaning where there may be none or it is too well hidden.

When your child recounts a dream to you, try to determine both the type of dream they have experienced and the meaning behind images and events by asking them questions related to key areas, which may be summarized in the following DREAM key:

DREAM KEY

DETAIL What details stand out in your child's recollections?

RECOGNITION Did your child recognize people, places or feelings in their dream?

EMOTIONS What was the overriding emotion experienced during the course of the dream?

ACTION Did your child take an active or passive role in their dream?

MEANING What does your child think the dream means?

How to Use this Book

The Dream Finder (*see pages 20–117*) contains real case examples of children's dreams from each of the three dream categories: positive childhood development dreams; creative and fantastic dreams; and nightmares and problem dreams. When exploring your child's dream you might like to look through the Dream Finder with your child to see if any of the dreams recounted there are similar in feeling, theme or context to the dream your child has just recounted. Take note if your child responds strongly to any of the images accompanying the relevant dreams in this section.

The dreams contained in the Dream Finder are also very useful for understanding how to use key questions to explore your child's dream and dreamercises to help your child get the most from dreaming. In many cases, the meanings of similar or related themes are also provided. Look through the dreamercises (*see pages 118–25*) to see if any are appropriate to your child's situation regarding their dream. Would they like to replay the dream another night (*see Dream Replay, page 119*) or do they need to rid themselves of a demon (*see Bash the Baddy, page 124*)? So your child can

keep a diary of their own dreams, I suggest you keep photocopies of the Dream Diary pages (*126–29*) by their bed.

Use the Dream Directory (*see pages 130–41*) to help you interpret the meaning behind specific imagery. This section contains some of the common images and symbols found in children's dreams and their possible meanings. Always bear in mind the context in which a particular image occurred and the attitude of your child towards it when trying to understand the symbolism of the image. Also, try to relate the meanings provided in the directory to what is happening in your child's life at the time of the dream.

This book is meant to encourage creative communication between you and your child. Use the ideas contained within it as a starting point for understanding your child's dreams and nurturing the development of their own unique personality. Follow your intuition and judgement when analysing their dreams and take care not to impose a significant meaning where there is none. Devise your own dreamercises to suit your child, and construct activities for encouraging your child's creativity and personal development, and for improving your relationship with one another.

Dream Finder

In the Dream Finder I have gathered together twenty-four dreams related by children aged between four and eleven. Each dream is illustrated and contains key questions, analysis and possible ways of using the dream to help nurture the child's personal development, encourage their creativity or simply give them pleasure. In many cases a specific dream-ercise is included and related themes are highlighted.

The dreams in the Dream Finder, which cover a wide range of themes and childhood issues, are grouped according to type of dream: reality-based, positive development dreams (*see pages 22–49*), creative and fantastic dreams (*see pages 50–69*), and nightmares and problem dreams (*see pages 70–117*). Familiarize yourself with all three categories by reading through all the dreams in the Dream Finder before beginning to interpret your child's dreams.

To enable you to identify which dream case study most closely resembles your child's, the theme and childhood marker of each dream in the Dream Finder are outlined at right. When your child relates their dream to you, first decide which category it belongs to and then read through the key characteristics of the dreams in that category to find the dream study that is most similar to your child's in one of its key aspects.

You may find that one of the dreams is similar in theme. For example, if your child has a reality-based, positive dream about sitting and 'doing' something, you may wish to look at Sally's dream (*see page 30*) for insight into the possible meanings of your child's dream and guidance on how to use it to benefit them. If you feel your child is at a developmental turning point, you may prefer to look at the critical childhood markers listed to see if any correspond to your child's stage of development. If you find a match here, even if the theme of the dream is completely different, you may still find the analysis of that dream helpful.

DREAM CASE STUDIES

Reality-based, Positive Development Dreams

Hanna's dream, page 22
Theme: climbing up castle steps
Childhood marker: 4–5 years; personality characteristics

Juan's dream, page 26:
Theme: playing happily with unusual detail (developing new interests)
Childhood marker: rapidly changing interests; seizing the moment

Sally's dream, page 30:
Theme: sitting doing a task
Childhood marker: 2–6 years; mastering new tasks

Sophie's dream, page 34:
Theme: looking over a fence into a garden
Childhood marker: natural curiosity; the 'why' stage

Sam's dream, page 38:
Theme: swimming through water
Childhood marker: surges in motivation

Kiren's dream, page 42:
Theme: marching in a parade
Childhood marker: developing refined social skills

Will's dream, page 46:
Theme: exploring a fantastic fort
Childhood marker: forging lasting friendships

Creative and Fantastic Dreams

Antonio's dream, page 50:
Theme: flying in a shooting rocket
Childhood marker: desire to be unique self

Stephie's dream, page 54:
Theme: being in a colorful, delightful, 'rainbowland'
Childhood marker: development of creative personality

Steven's dream, page 58:
Theme: adventures in an amazing theme park
Childhood marker: striving to keep up with older siblings

Gabriella's dream, page 62:
Theme: running through a beautiful wood
Childhood marker: personality of only child

Jenny's dream, page 66:
Theme: weird and wonderful shop setting
Childhood marker: pre-teen; emotional separation from parents

Nightmares and Problem Dreams

Jack's dream, page 70:
Theme: sitting at the top of a tree feeling unhappy
Childhood marker: 3–4 years; night-time toilet training

Jane's dream, page 74:
Theme: wearing a favorite party dress that had become different
Childhood marker: adjusting to a parent's new partner

Adriana's dream, page 78:
Theme: trapped inside a big, rolling ball
Childhood marker: adapting to major changes

Jason's dream, page 82:
Theme: racing through a garden with monster-like plants
Childhood marker: facing social problems such as bullying

Zoe's dream, page 86:
Theme: chasing a pet (in reality, dead) in the dark
Childhood marker: learning about loss

Andrew's dream, page 90:
Theme: playing in an empty, frightening building
Childhood marker: feeling 'behind' in school work

Chloe's dream, page 94:
Theme: panicking over loss of favorite jumper
Childhood marker: fear of abandonment by parent after divorce

Derek's dream, page 98:
Theme: pots and pans fall out of a cupboard on top of child
Childhood marker: dealing with pressure from parents to succeed

Samantha's dream, page 102:
Theme: doll undergoes disturbing changes
Childhood marker: learning to handle difficulties in friendships

Tiffany's dream, page 106:
Theme: frightening experience in a classroom
Childhood marker: dealing with the negative effects of a thoughtless teacher

Alex's dream, page 110:
Theme: frightening man at the end of the bed
Childhood marker: feelings of guilt about parental discord

Marco's dream, page 114:
Theme: feeling trapped and angry with no escape
Childhood marker: difficulty handling aggressive impulses

The Princess and the Castle

Hanna's dream, aged five

"I had a magical dream in which I was a lovely princess, climbing huge castle steps. The sky above me was a brilliant blue, the sun was shining and my dress was brightly colored. I wanted to get to the top of the castle steps. The castle had tall towers but I did not feel afraid. As I climbed up and up, the steps got larger. As they grew bigger I had to hold on to them tightly to pull myself up. "

The Dream Context

Hanna had recently started elementary school. Her mother, Jan, was aware of the normal fears children often have about going to 'big' school. She tried to make the first few weeks as positive as possible. And Hanna did seem happy, excitedly talking about the days' events and putting great effort into learning new skills. Jan wanted to find the right balance between encouraging Hanna enthusiastically and keeping the new challenges in perspective. She did not want Hanna to feel that she had to 'achieve' in order to please her family – Jan herself had felt under pressure to achieve academically as a child.

How Hanna Felt

Hanna vividly described the physical exertion of gripping and climbing, although the sense of joy she felt at achieving her goal – reaching the top – was evident. At the top of the steps Hanna recounted spreading her arms and twirling about happily, with her long sleeves flowing in the wind.

Key Questions

This is the perfect opportunity to make your child feel their dream was special and increase their self worth.

? What were you wearing? Can you describe it? Praise any use of detail.

? What did it feel like being a princess?

? What were the most important things about your castle? (Here substitute the main image in your child's dream.)

? Ask about any detail that stands out as it may hold key meaning: 'Hanna, what did it feel like when you gripped those large steps?'

Aim of Analysis

As this was an enchanting dream, Jan used it as a basis to meet three objectives:

1. To explore the 'good' things inspiring this dream in order to encourage these more.

2. To excite Hanna to the possibilities of adapting it creatively.

3. To encourage positive communication with Hanna and a friend.

Critical Childhood Marker

Starting primary school is a critical transition point in childhood. Enduring personality characteristics have been laid down, and these, in part, determine how well your child negotiates the new demands. An awareness of, for example, whether your child is shy or demanding, will give you an idea of where they may need help in adjusting. Their dreams will be a good indicator of their initial reaction to school.

What Hanna and Jan Did

Jan believed that Hanna was feeling good about herself. The castle description, large yet unthreatening, seemed to represent Hanna's attitude to school: positive and without anxiety. Even gripping large steps suggested that Hanna recognized the challenges but was taking them in her stride.

Jan decided that her enthusiastic approach was working and she would keep up the good work.

Jan put this dream to creative use. Together they made princess costumes and devised a small play.

Jan encouraged Hanna to enlist a friend to help with the play. The two girls had a wonderful time pretending to be princesses.

Dreamercise

If your child has a particularly nice dream, help them to revisit it with the power of suggestion:

At bedtime suggest they recount main parts of the dream and how they felt.

Ask them if they'd like to revisit it. Tell them to close their eyes and picture the vivid images they remember.

As they settle down quietly suggest, 'Hanna I can see you as a beautiful princess, in the sunshine, climbing up and up to your very own beautiful castle ...'

RELATED THEMES

• **Palaces and Grand Buildings** Non-threatening, complicated buildings usually represent natural curiosity. Try some creative, fun activities (*see page 45*).

• **Climbing Trees or Ropes** Is your child facing a challenge? If climbing is a struggle, then be aware of how they are coping. They may need extra support.

• **Scaling Walls or Fences** Is your child facing a minor problem? Try asking gently about schoolwork and observe them around the house. See if one area seems to be causing worry.

Swinging on a Tree, Shoes Full of Shells

Juan's dream, aged six

"**I** was jumping up and down in sand. With a big jump I sailed up into the air and grabbed the lowest branch of a tree. The branch was made of rocks. I started swinging – it was great. I watched my big shoes go up in front of me and then disappear behind me. They seemed to be full of shells. I wanted to jump down, take them off and get all the shells out. I landed in the sand and started to pick all the rocks off the branch. My pockets were getting full and I wondered if the shells came from the sand.**"

26

The Dream Context

Juan is an only child and a fairly quiet boy. His mother, Maria, has always found it a little difficult to chat to him and would like to find ways to communicate with him better. Recently, his grandmother had taken Juan to the local museum. Although he hadn't said much about the visit, his grandmother remarked that she couldn't move him away from the fossil collection. The dream seemed to show that a real interest in fossils, rocks and shells had been stimulated.

How Juan Felt

In his dream, Juan felt calm and on familiar territory (he has a sandbox in his garden). After jumping in the sand his excitement mounted when he saw the rocks in the branch – evident in the animated way he recounted this part of the dream. He felt that he could not wait to get the shells out of his shoes. That the shells were in his shoes demonstrated how very 'close to home' his interest was. He revealed his curiosity when he wondered if the shells came from the sand.

Key Questions

Such a dream gives you an exciting chance to open up communication with a quiet child.

? How did it feel when you were jumping?

? What were you thinking when your dream changed from jumping to swinging?

? Were the rocks colourful? Did the shells have patterns?

? Do you think the sand contained more treasures? (Here substitute the image in your child's dream that contained hidden treasure, for example, a box or container.)

Aim of Analysis

Maria wanted to use Juan's dream to develop a number of ideas; for example:

1. To open up new ways of communicating with him, using his new-found interest.

2. To build up his confidence in communicating with others by helping him to develop his interest in rocks and fossils.

3. To form the basis of a day out to remember.

Critical Childhood Marker

Children's interests can change rapidly, so it is important to seize the moment when they dream of something that could become a hobby. Sometimes interests are directly related to a developmental stage of childhood; for example, your child might dream about reading a book when they are in the 'reading readiness' stage. Other interests arise spontaneously or as a direct result of a particular experience. Suddenly they can talk of nothing but dinosaurs. A chance remark, or glimpse of an image in a book or on television can spark an interest.

What Juan and Maria Did

Maria felt that Juan's dream emphasized his general contentment with life. He had enjoyed jumping in the pile of sand and had found swinging on the branch and making the discoveries about the rocks and shells exciting. His 'big' shoes reflected his confidence about making discoveries – he had truly found something that interested him and 'fit' with his expectations. If his shoes had been falling off his feet they might have indicated anxiety.

Maria asked Juan if he would like a day out at the beach digging for fossils. He jumped at the chance and chattered excitedly about what they would need. This naturally opened up a conversation for them. Plan a day out that encourages your child's new interest.

Juan's father helped him put together a collector's bag for any new discoveries. Juan decided what he wanted to put into it – a small spade, a pick, tissues, some plastic bags.

Together they looked at a book about rocks and minerals. Maria asked Juan if any of the rocks looked like the ones in his dream.

Juan drew pictures of the shells from his dream and described them.

Dreamercise

If you are trying to establish more active communication with your child try the 'Adventurous journey' dreamercise (see page 121), relating it to the subject of your child's dream.

⏰ At bedtime ask your child where the most exciting place in the world is, then look it up on a map.

⏰ Discuss what they think it would be like; the more adventurous their ideas, the better.

⏰ Suggest to them, as they climb into bed, that they can take an adventurous journey there in their dreams.

Making Grass Patterns

Sally's dream, aged four

"I was sitting in the garden, which was lovely and warm. The grass was very long – not like ours. I pulled some grass out and looked over my shoulder to see if anyone was watching. Then I started making a pattern with the grass. I twisted some pieces over each other. They looked pretty but they didn't look 'right'. So I picked some more of the long grass. It was very green and felt slippery. I started making a pattern again and then my friend Janie walked into the garden and I lost my grass pieces!"

How Sally Felt

Sally's basic feeling of contentment was evident in her description of the lovely, warm garden. She viewed trying to make patterns with the grass as a duty, likening the task to tidying her room. That the grass did not look 'right' indicated her dissatisfaction, and the slippery quality of the grass suggested that Sally found manipulating it tricky. Although she did not feel unduly disturbed during the dream, her disappointment at losing the grass pieces was clear when she was distracted by her friend Janie.

The Dream Context

Sally had recently been trying to tie her shoe laces. Her mother, Helen, noticed that sometimes she would happily get as far as she could and then look up expectantly at her parents to finish the job. Other days Sally would become exasperated with her inability to tie them, kick off her shoes and storm into her bedroom. Once she walked into the kitchen with mock pride, pretending that she had tied her laces correctly even though the loops were already slipping apart. She and her father had had a good giggle. Helen wanted to help Sally learn to tie her own shoe laces but was wary of taking over from her.

Critical Childhood Marker

A large part of the first five years of life consists of learning practical tasks, from tying your shoe laces to brushing your teeth. Success in learning such tasks depends to a large extent on the encouragement your child receives. When your child seems ready to learn a new task, offer them positive help and lots of praise, and acknowledge when something is too difficult for them to manage at the moment.

Aim of Analysis

Sally's dream clearly related to learning a new task – in this case, tying her shoe laces. It offered Helen the opportunity to find out if she was helping her child manage this task appropriately.

1 It gave Helen scope to bolster Sally's confidence in her practical abilities.

2 It opened the door for some enjoyable creative play, which had practical applications.

3 It helped Helen decide how she might spend extra time with Sally.

What Sally and Helen Did

Although the tenor of the dream was positive, Helen felt that Sally's dream contained mixed feelings. Only by exploring them could she tease out how positively Sally was feeling about learning her current task. The garden was 'lovely and warm', indicating that Sally felt comfortable within her family, but the fact that she had looked over her shoulder revealed how much she sensed that people were watching her progress.

Helen took this as a cue to downplay any time Sally failed to tie her shoelaces. She also discouraged Sally's older sister and brother from commenting unless it was to remark on Sally's successes.

No one had told Sally to make grass patterns in her dream, revealing a high level of self-motivation. Helen thought she would emphasize the creative aspect of the

Key Questions

A dream like Sally's offers the chance to understand an important aspect of child development. Helen wanted to explore Sally's feelings about tying her shoe laces.

? How did it feel playing with the long grass?

? Did it remind you of anything?

? Why did you look over your shoulder? (Here substitute where your child was looking in their dream.)

? Did you think Janie was coming to play?

32

task by giving her some brightly colored strings to weave and plait. Not only was this fun but it also helped Sally's growing hand-eye co-ordination.

Helen asked Sally to describe her garden in more detail. Then – to make her feel special – she suggested gluing the brightly colored strings on to some green paper to make a garden picture for the kitchen wall.

Helen set aside a special time for shoe-lace tying when no one else was about.

RELATED THEMES

Doing things with their hands frequently occurs in children's dreams, perhaps because so much learning and creative work involves their hands.

• **Things Slipping Through the Hands** Generally means your child is fearful of something. Explore what is slipping through their hands to discover clues to their fears.

• **Trying to Grasp with the Hands** Reveals the motivation to accomplish a particular task or skill. Discover and encourage what they are trying to learn in waking life.

• **Twisting the Hands** Your child may be anxious about something that is happening in the family or at school. This is similar to wringing the hands when awake.

• **Cupping Something with the Hands** Indicates that your child is treasuring something. Whatever they are cupping may represent 'feelings' or an actual person or animal – perhaps a much-loved pet.

A Garden Full of Wonder

Sophie's dream, aged four

"I was in a very sunny place, looking over a fence. It was wooden and a bit splintery. Over the fence were beautiful flowers lined up in pots. They were all my favorite colors as well as colors I don't know the names of. They were so big, too. Bees were buzzing around in bee 'families', all moving together. They seemed to dance on the petals. I wanted to smell the flowers but my nose wouldn't go any further over the fence. Some of the bees swooshed away and I waved to them. They went into the sky. I wanted to ask their names."

How Sophie Felt

Sophie was clearly excited when describing the dream. She seemed particularly enthralled by the size and colors of the flowers and the 'friendly' bee families. Sophie took great pleasure in describing the 'swooshing' of the bees and how she wanted to 'chat' to them. The only negative aspects of this otherwise highly positive dream were Sophie's description of the splinters on the fence – indicating that she felt a little inhibited by its presence – and the fact that she could not smell the flowers.

The Dream Context

Recently Sophie had been asking her mother, Susan, a constant stream of 'why' questions. Susan thought that Sophie had been through the 'why' stage when she was three when Sophie had wanted to know every last detail about every event. Although Susan had felt exasperated, she had resisted telling Sophie to stop asking, always trying to be the 'good' mom. Now it was starting again and Susan did not know how she was going to answer the latest incessant questioning without sounding completely impatient.

Key Questions

Sophie's dream and her keen desire to recount it presented Susan with a wealth of starting points for asking questions. Such intelligence means you can put your younger child in the driving seat.

? What are your favorite colors? Shall we look in your color book so you can show me the ones that you didn't know the names of?

? Do you think bees can be friendly? Do you think they live in families?

? What did it feel like peering over the splintery fence?

? Did you wish you could 'swoosh' away with the bees?

Critical Childhood Marker

A child's natural curiosity develops from early infancy through stimulation of the senses – vision, taste, touch, hearing and smell. The walking and early talking of toddlerhood develops into the 'why' stages of the three to fives. At this point many parents quash their child's wonder at life without realizing it. They moan: 'Not another question!' Resist this temptation. If you are busy say: 'What a great question, let's talk about it at lunch.' The happiest and most creative adults are those who never stopped wondering 'why' about the nature and variety of life.

Aim of Analysis

This dream clearly demonstrated Sophie's natural curiosity, giving Susan the chance to re-evaluate how she treated Sophie's 'why' questions.

1. It gave Susan many ideas for developing Sophie's interests further.

2. It provided a natural introduction to information and reference books.

3. It offered Sophie some great themes for colorful drawings.

What Sophie and Susan Did

Sophie's dream made Susan realize just how exciting Sophie found the world right now. Clearly Sophie felt excited in the dream if a little frustrated. Susan understood that the splintery fence reflected her prickly attitude towards Sophie's endless questions. The dream prompted Susan to feel very warm towards Sophie and a touch guilty at her own impatience.

The *Key Question* Susan posed to Sophie about colors led to an excited look through Sophie's coloring book. Sophie soon identified the colors in her dream that she did not know the names of and memorized them.

At Sophie's insistence they also visited the library to find books about bees. Sophie's eagerness to go to the library indicated just how critical this particular point was in her development.

Susan and Sophie had fun with the word 'swoosh'.

By using your child's own words when talking to them you show you are really listening to them.

Sophie had great fun drawing bold and beautiful pictures of 'her' garden and bees.

Sophie and Susan talked about the way flowers smell. They took Sophie's creativity to another level when Susan asked her what sorts of exciting smells the flowers might have. 'Like peppermint!' was Sophie's first response.

RELATED THEMES

• **Fences in Nightmares** Fences can be protective. In a nightmare, children with problems sometimes create a protective 'ring' around themselves in the form of a fence. Fences can also be exclusive. The child dreaming cannot get over the fence into a safe zone away from the nightmare.

• **Looking Through Fences** If your child is looking through a fence, and reports a sense of anxiety, they may feel left out – of their circle of friends, at school, or within the family.

• **Balancing on Fences** You may have a little daredevil on your hands if your child is teetering on top of a fence and reports a sense of excitement. If frightened, they may feel under pressure.

• **Getting Stuck Under a Fence** Your child feels threatened – it's a scary feeling being trapped. They may need to sort something out: some gentle questioning from you may help them do so.

Swimming Strongly towards Success

Sam's dream, aged ten

> "I was swimming under water. It was quite dark and I could see light from the sky above. I seemed to be able to hold my breath for ages. I did want to reach the surface, though. At first my legs and arms didn't seem to work properly. But as I tried harder, they began to pull together and suddenly I was swimming at a real pace. My right hand broke through the surface of the water, although my left hand couldn't quite break through. There were other swimmers beside me now and we all headed in the same direction."

38

The Dream Context

Sam is the middle child of three. His parents had always found him outwardly easy going but his father, George, had often worried that he might feel a little left out at times. Lately he had been trying particularly hard at anything presented to him, from mastering his older sister's new computer game to playing football for the school. George wondered if Sam's determination to succeed was a sign of insecurity – that he was battling for attention through his 'performance'.

Critical Childhood Marker

Children experience periodic surges in motivation and drive, particularly when faced with a challenge. Starting a new school or sitting exams can bring out the best in those children with a high level of self-confidence. Others find such hurdles more difficult to cope with.

The determination of the very young to walk and to climb can be quite startling to parents. In older children the same determination can sometimes pass unnoticed when a little reassurance or encouragement would help sustain their drive.

How Sam Felt

Sam described pushing through the water with great feeling, amazed that he could hold his breath for so long. Sam felt he could have gone on swimming forever, although the desire to reach the surface and the light above it had been very strong. Once his right hand had broken the surface Sam felt some frustration that his left hand – the one he relied on in waking life – could not do the same. Being joined by the other swimmers made him feel that they were sharing this strange experience.

Key Questions

George hoped to understand Sam's feelings about what others expected of him and what he expected of himself.

? Where did you think you were and how did it feel?

? Do you think the water represented something in your life? (Ask a younger child if the water reminds them of something.)

? Why do you think your left hand couldn't break through?

? Did the feeling of making your arms and legs work together seem familiar?

Aim of Analysis

Sam's dream contained a lot of symbolism, which George used to achieve the following goals:

1 To determine if Sam was feeling fine within himself about the way he was meeting the challenges in his life.

2 To reduce any feeling Sam might have of being left out within the family by giving him some one-to-one time.

3 To help him to focus his drive and determination.

What Sam and George Did

It was important to George to use this opportunity to explore Sam's sense of well being.

Simply by talking with him George found that his son was excited by what was happening in his life. Sam loved the football team at school and – unbeknown to George – had signed up for a swimming gala for charity. Now the water made sense. Sam did not seem too concerned that his older sister's upcoming exams dominated family life. He simply wanted to get on with his own life.

That his left hand was unable to penetrate the surface of the water led George to believe that maybe he had been complacent about letting Sam get on with everything by himself. He decided to give Sam active encouragement every week.

They talked about school. Sam had been assigned a short story for creative writing. George suggested that he base it on the adventures of a long-distance swimmer. Sam thought it would be great if the swimmer became separated from his 'supply' boat.

RELATED THEMES

Water is a common element in dreams, sometimes threatening, sometimes pleasurable. Pay particular attention to your child's feelings about the water.

• **Jumping into Water without Fear** This represents a sense of joy. It resembles the toddlerhood pleasure of stomping in puddles.

• **Sinking in Water** This can indicate anxiety. Does your child feel unable to cope with something? Perhaps they feel they are being left behind at school or by their friends.

• **Whirling or Being Swallowed Up by Water** Your child is frightened of something. They are literally 'drowning' in negative emotions. Explore what this might relate to.

• **Being Rained On** Are you being negative with your child? They may feel drenched with criticism.

The Leader of the Parade

Kiren's dream, aged eight

"I found myself marching in a parade full of fantastic floats! Most people were in really cool animal costumes. Suddenly I was swooped up on to the biggest float at the front of the parade. There was a chair just for me! I got on the chair and I could see all around. Loads of people were watching and I felt really excited. Everyone on my float was dressed as a cat. I was like the 'Queen cat'. The parade stopped and someone asked me which way to go. I carefully looked around, then I chose a winding road."

The Dream Context

Kiren was the oldest of four children. Her mother, Jamila, had separated amicably from Kiren's father and needed Kiren to help organize the younger ones. Jamila wondered if perhaps she was giving Kiren too much responsibility. Even before the marriage broke down, Jamila would call Kiren her 'little filofax' because she was so organized. Kiren seemed a fairly confident child and Jamila hoped that she had not passed on her personal sense of failure over the divorce to her daughter.

How Kiren Felt

Kiren's excitement as she described her dream was evident. There was an exuberance that delighted Jamila. Kiren's descriptions of the costumes were very detailed and realistic. Kiren loved the 'swooping' sensation that landed her on top of the float and adored her special chair. In telling of her choice of direction, Kiren emanated a thoughtful rather than a bossy air. There was a sense that her decision took into account what everyone in the parade would want.

Key Questions

Kiren's dream gave Jamila the chance to explore how Kiren felt about her responsibilities at home and her attitude towards her friends.

? What did you think when you found yourself in the parade? (Here substitute the activity your child joined.)

? How did you know the chair was for you? (Here substitute the object in your child's dream that seemed to be theirs.)

? Why do you think everyone on your float were cats and how did it feel to be 'Queen cat'?

? What made you choose that particular road?

Aim of Analysis

Some children seem to have a natural resilience to family problems. Jamila used Kiren's dream to meet the following objectives:

1. To determine the extent to which the positive atmosphere of Kiren's dream reflected her waking life.

2. To reassure herself that Kiren was coping with her new responsibilities.

3. To encourage the development of Kiren's natural leadership abilities.

4. To enable Kiren to enjoy some creative time with the family.

What Kiren and Jamila Did

Talking about Kiren's dream made Jamila realize just how well adjusted Kiren was in terms of the separation. Kiren was enthusiastic about the parade: such a vibrant image suggested a life being lived to the full. The excitement she felt about her special chair and role as 'Queen cat' represented Kiren's natural desire to be in control, while the pause she took to consider which road to take revealed her thoughtfulness about the others in the parade.

Kiren's enthusiasm for the cat costumes paved the way for creative activity. Kiren wanted to make a cat costume for Halloween. Jamila suggested she ask her grandmother, who was good at dressmaking, to help her make it.

Critical Childhood Marker

Some of the more subtle social skills are developed by children to different degrees depending on personality and life experiences. Leadership skills belong to this category. Does your child have plenty of ideas and the ability to interest their friends in them?

Your child may develop leadership qualities through being given responsibilities at home or school. Alternatively, the sheer force of your child's personality may incline them to be leader of the 'gang'. Reinforcing your child's belief in themselves will encourage the development of this skill and help them to say 'no' to activities they feel are wrong.

Kiren was monitor for the junior gymnastics club. Jamila asked Kiren what she did if any of the other girls dragged their feet. Kiren's solution was to ask them how they would organize the gym equipment: that is, she involved them in the decision-making process. Jamila praised Kiren's natural insight.

Jamila decided it was important to maintain Kiren's confidence level. She encouraged Kiren's father to praise her helping at home with the younger children. Even if he was not there to see it, Kiren would still feel he was interested in her everyday life.

Kiren had fun organizing the three younger children into a makeshift parade. Jamila put out some special treats for them to enjoy.

Dreamercise

Kiren had so enjoyed telling Jamila about her dream that Jamila suggested trying the 'dream replay' dreamercise (see page 119).

🕐 At bedtime she asked Kiren to recount in detail her 'parade' dream.

🕐 'Remind me what the cat costumes looked like,' Jamila said.

🕐 She suggested that Kiren replay the dream but this time allow the parade to carry on up the road she chose. Where would it finish – in some wonderful place?

Building Solid Friendships

Will's dream, aged seven

"I was in a fantastic fort. I was at the top level with some other children. We were talking excitedly but I don't remember what about. Suddenly we were standing at a strange little window in a turret. It was a lookout. We were sharing it, taking turns peering out. I could see woods but nothing in them. Another boy was saying, 'Look harder, look harder!' I wasn't sure what to look for. Then someone shouted that the wall should be checked to make sure it was safe. Several of us started feeling it for cracks."

The Dream Context

Will had recently started playing with a new group of friends at school. His mother, Victoria, was concerned that he was moving on to a new group of friends because he had not been fully accepted by the last one. She had noticed how selfish he could be, especially with his younger brother, and worried that because of this he would be unable to develop long-lasting friendships. Victoria had found it hard making friends as a child and did not want Will to have the same experience.

How Will Felt

Will talked about his dream with great excitement. Clearly, exploring the fort had been enjoyable. He did not find being with the other children threatening, and seemed happy to take turns peering through the lookout. In fact, he seemed positively to enjoy this activity. Although Will was a little concerned about 'missing' what the other boy could see in the woods, his dream ended positively with all the children 'in it together', checking the wall.

Key Questions

Victoria used the following questions to explore the way Will felt about making friends.

? Was it good to be in the fort with the other children?

? What did it feel like taking turns at the lookout?

? Did you like the children's company?

? What do you think the boy wanted you to see? (Here, substitute what another child was asking your child to do.)

? What did the wall feel like? (Here, substitute the surface your child was touching in their dream.)

Aim of Analysis

Victoria wanted to be sure that Will was happy in himself when interacting with friends. She used the dream as the basis for achieving the following goals:

1 To understand how Will felt in his new social group. Victoria could 'check' this against her own childhood feelings about making friends.

2 To develop better communication between herself and Will, and between Will and his younger brother.

3 To actively encourage some fun activities for Will and his new friends.

What Will and Victoria Did

Victoria was very pleased to find that Will felt positively about his dream – he had obviously begun to really enjoy his friendships. However, his inability to 'see' exactly what the other boy saw conveyed a degree of insecurity about his new friendships which Victoria wanted to help remove.

After talking excitedly about the dream Victoria asked Will to suggest a fun day out with his friends. He asked if he could invite them to the adventure playground across town.

They talked about how good it felt to take turns. Victoria reminded Will of the time his uncle had let him go first on the diving board at the swimming baths. She asked Will if his little brother might feel the same about being allowed 'first turn' sometimes.

Dreamercise

You can encourage the development of a particular skill by using the Happy Moments dreamercise (*see page 118*).

🕐 At bedtime she asked Will to think of the best moment he had shared with his little brother. Will told her about the time he had shared a tub of ice cream with him.

🕐 Victoria asked Will to describe the flavor of the ice cream, and the time and place of this happy moment. She suggested that he revisit that happy moment in his dreams, and commented that perhaps his dream fort had been protecting an ice-cream factory.

Critical Childhood Marker

The finer social skills required to forge close, lasting friendships, such as taking turns and listening to others' ideas, usually develop between the ages of seven and nine. At about this time children begin to understand that the best way to maintain friendships is not necessarily to act on their immediate impulses or to do exactly what they want to do irrespective of what anybody else would like to do!

Victoria asked Will to reconstruct his dream fort with his bricks. Delighted, Will used his toy soldiers to show her how the children were positioned in his dream.

Victoria showed Will a picture of the Tower of London and asked Will to point to any features that also appeared in his fort. They also discussed visiting a famous fort a few miles away.

Rocket to the Moon

Antonio's dream, aged eight

"I was in a rocket shooting fast through the air. It was great watching outer space fly past the windows. We were aiming to go to the moon and as it approached it looked huge. We started to circle it — we shot around and around at great speed. Someone shouted to me to look back 'home'. Home was the Earth. We could see cars and things that seemed really strange. How could we see them when we were so far away? It was the most magic feeling — I thought anything could happen."

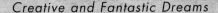

How Antonio Felt

Antonio described a sense of excitement and wonder in his dream. He found it thrilling travelling through space to the Moon. At no time did he feel any fear or anxiety about being in the rocket. Antonio was so excited when he told his mother, Emmy, about his dream over breakfast that she joked, 'Maybe you'll be an astronaut!'

The Dream Context

Antonio is a lively boy with an equally lively imagination, which sometimes dismayed his mother. For example, when he was supposed to be doing his schoolwork he would often suddenly ask about something that seemed completely unrelated or describe an adventure he would like to have. Keeping him focused on the everyday was becoming harder and harder. On the positive side, when the family was relaxing together, Antonio often kept them entertained with his huge store of ideas and plans. 'Maybe he'll be an inventor,' his father, Andreas, would laugh.

Critical Childhood Marker

It is easy to ignore a child's wilder fantasies or crazy ideas. Parents roll their eyes and ask, 'Where did they come up with that?' However, if your child demonstrates a natural *joie de vie* be sure to nurture it. At school they may not get much encouragement and they need the freedom to enjoy their flights of fancy to develop their creativity. Often the quirkiest children are the happiest individuals.

By the age of three, a child's personality begins to stand out clearly. By the age of eight – Antonio's age – their idiosyncracies and preferences, dreams and expectations are fully evident, and you can delight in their individuality!

Aim of Analysis

Emmy found Antonio's enthusiasm contagious as he talked about his dream. Suddenly she saw a lively little boy describing something he felt excited about and she realized that this shared moment could be used to:

1. Build his confidence in himself and generate some closeness between them.
2. Communicate to him what a special person she thought he was.
3. Put the dream to work for him in a fun and creative way.

What Antonio and Emmy Did

The content of the dream – rocket, crew, Moon and Earth – provided many talking points. The key questions led to more intriguing questions.

Simply giving Antonio the time and attention to describe his dream fully is a natural confidence booster. Children love to think they have something to share that an adult finds interesting.

As he talked, Antonio described an invention he thought would help astronauts on space missions. Emmy praised his ingenuity and suggested he start an inventor's notebook to keep his ideas in. This made Antonio feel important.

Asking a simple question like 'Were you in charge of the rocket?' gives your child the sense that they can be in charge. Because mom or dad thinks it is

Key Questions

When your child excitedly relates a fantastic dream, use it to develop their memory, pleasure and communication.

? Were you in a space suit? (Here, substitute the detail that would apply in your child's dream.)

? Were you in charge of the rocket?

? What did you see in outer space?

? What color was the Moon? Was anything on the Moon?

Dreamercise

This was the perfect opportunity to use the Dream Replay dreamercise (*see page 119*). Because Antonio had so enjoyed his dream, why not revisit it?

🕰 *Emmy suggested they look at Antonio's drawings of rockets at bedtime. Antonio was happy to talk about them.*

🕰 *Next Emmy asked him to retell his wonderful dream to her. She emphasized how much she enjoyed listening to him.*

🕰 *As she put his drawings away and tucked him in, she asked where he might go in his wonderful dream rocket tonight. 'To Mars!' he replied excitedly.*

possible, they feel complimented and their confidence is increased.

Emmy asked if Antonio's science teacher had any books about space. Perhaps he would show them to Antonio? Or they could pay a visit to the library.

Antonio said he was going to design and build a space rocket in his arts and crafts lesson. Emmy suggested he draw the rocket from his dream before he forgot any of the details. Being involved in this way encourages your child.

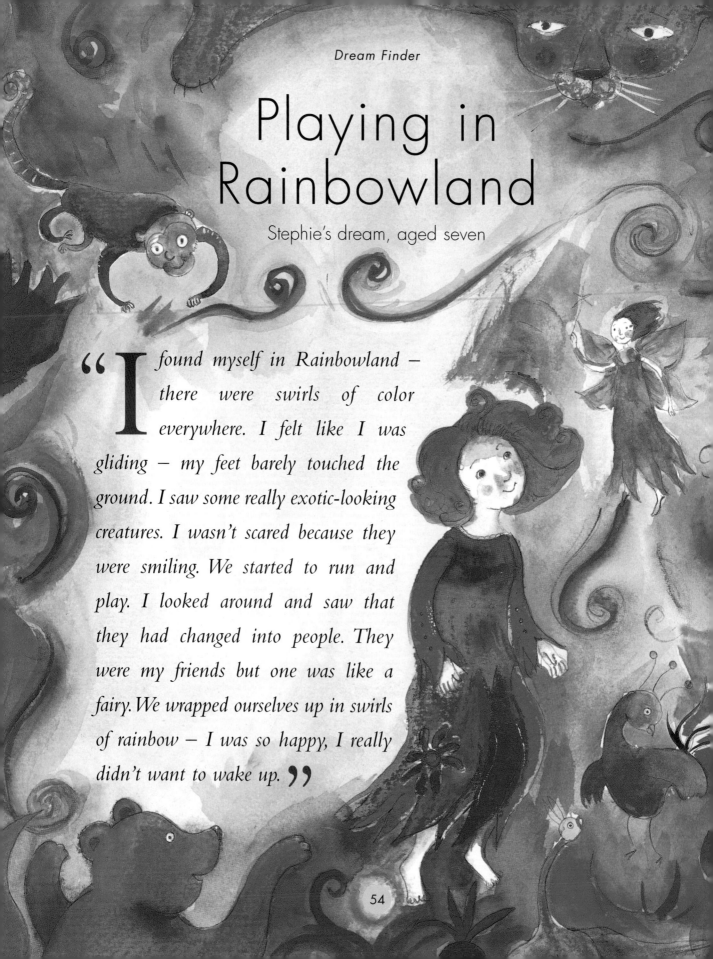

Playing in Rainbowland

Stephie's dream, aged seven

"*I found myself in Rainbowland — there were swirls of color everywhere. I felt like I was gliding — my feet barely touched the ground. I saw some really exotic-looking creatures. I wasn't scared because they were smiling. We started to run and play. I looked around and saw that they had changed into people. They were my friends but one was like a fairy. We wrapped ourselves up in swirls of rainbow — I was so happy, I really didn't want to wake up.*"

Key Questions

Serena wanted to explore the wonderful creativity of Stephie's fantastical dream.

? Could you feel the swirls of color?

? What was it like to float?

? What did the friendly creatures look like?

? What sorts of games were you playing?

? Did the fairy have a name?

How Stephie Felt

Stephie felt glorious after her amazing dream. The first thing she did on waking was run into her parents' bedroom and describe her dream to them. She delighted in the colors, swirls and patterns. The exotic creatures that became people held particular interest for her. She said how great it was that some friends joined her in 'Rainbowland'. Stephie wondered aloud whether other children had such dreams.

The Dream Context

Stephie enjoyed playing with her friends. Her mother, Serena, was pleased that she did not suffer from shyness but worried that Stephie was over-sensitive, sometimes hurt by other's remarks. Stephie's father, Nick, believed that she would develop along the path her spirit took her.

Aim of Analysis

By spending time talking with Stephie about her dream, Serena hoped to develop some creative communication. She wanted to:

1. Use the dream as a starting point for some creative free-association.
2. Find out how Stephie would like to use the images in her dream for some art projects.
3. Develop some fun ideas for Stephie's upcoming birthday party.

What Stephie and Serena Did

Serena shared some very warm moments with Stephie simply by listening to her. The key questions allowed Stephie some unrestrained thinking about the entire sensory experience. Positive developments occurred.

Stephie told her mother that the fairy's name was Sally Tinkerbell, and declared that she would write a story about her. Stephie drew some colourful and lively pictures of Sally Tinkerbell.

When asked about the story she would write, Stephie came up with a wide variety of adventures her fairy could have. All Sally Tinkerbell's adventures would be set in 'Rainbowland'.

For her birthday Stephie suggested a fairy party. Her friends could come in fairy costumes. She also wanted to invite the new girl at school because 'she gets left out'. For the event,

Critical Childhood Marker

It is easy to become overly concerned about your child's emotional, social or academic development. Your child's first day at school or first exam can cause anxiety, as may particular aspects of your child's developing personality.

However, unless your child has special needs, all they really need is lots of love and attention. Even the most contented child has to endure occasional knocks, climb one or two hurdles and learn a few lessons of life. You should not worry too much unless your child finds it hard to bounce back.

Stephie suggested making fairy cakes covered in rainbow colors and decorating the room with rainbow colors.

Serena felt reassured that Stephie was happy and confident in herself. She also realized that her daughter's sensitivity had a positive aspect: it kept her in tune with others' feelings and enabled her to find the special in people.

RELATED THEMES

Sometimes fantastical dreams seem just that — a wonderful collection of exciting images. However, some images may relate to your child's development or show just how creative they are.

• **Creatures that Become People** If there is some anxiety attached to this image than your child may be thrown by the unexpected. Encourage their adventurous side.

• **Colorful Scenes** If colors dominate the dream, use them as the basis of some creative work — you may have a budding painter. Some children say they dream in black and white, not finding such dreams particularly exciting. Suggest painting their dreams with a rainbow — this can help develop their creativity.

• **Sunny Landscapes** Your child is feeling happy and positive at the moment.

• **Feet not Touching the Ground** Your child is 'flying' through this period of life unless there is some anxiety attached, in which case they may feel out of control.

All the Fun of the Fair

Steven's dream, aged seven

"I was in a tunnel that made me feel dizzy. I followed my brother's voice and came into an amazing underground theme park. My brother was hanging from a parachute ride. He was calling out to me to join him. Then I saw my father in a capsule-type ride. He was saying: 'Hop on.' I didn't know which ride to choose. Then I saw a big dipper ride; there were park staff on it, laughing and throwing sweets down on people below. I shouted: 'Take me!' They pulled me up and off the ride went."

The Dream Context

Steven was an excitable boy who was always trying to imitate his older brother, Sean, and constantly asking if he could do whatever his brother was doing. His parents tried to interest him in activities suitable for his age. But Steven could be determined and there were times when they found it difficult to prevent him from trying to keep up with his brother.

How Steven Felt

Steven felt like he had been allowed to run wild in a candy shop: there was so much going on, and it was all his for the taking. His sense of wonder came across very strongly. He had felt absolutely no fear. His parents were also struck that Steven had chosen his own ride rather than follow his brother, as they would have expected him to do. As his dream came to a close, Steven felt on top of the world, swooping in the big dipper.

Critical Childhood Marker

It is important not to have the same expectations for every child in the family. Siblings rarely develop at exactly the same pace and in the same way as each other and often have completely different personalities. Although it is quite natural for a younger child to want to imitate an older one, it is not always possible or appropriate for them to do so. At such times it is important to introduce them to an activity they can manage and enjoy or to explain that the older child has certain privileges that they will also enjoy when they reach the same age.

Aim of Analysis

Steven's mother, Eleanor, hoped to develop some creative, age-appropriate activities from this amazing dream. She wanted to achieve the following goals:

1 To use the dream as a springboard for some fun conversation.

2 To explore what sort of crafts Steven would enjoy doing.

3 To plan a special outing with only Steven, to give him some individual time.

What Steven and Eleanor Did

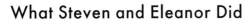

Eleanor took such pleasure in listening to Steven's dream that she decided to make a point of asking about her son's dreams on a regular basis in future.

Steven was such an active child they rarely sat and talked. However, his exciting dream stimulated conversation between them and they discussed all the amusing incidents that could have happened. The key questions emphasized Steven's role to such an extent that he said he 'knew his own ride was going to be the most exciting' and it was his 'special theme park, where no one was allowed without his permission'.

Eleanor asked what he could make from his dream. Steven asked if he could construct a 'dipper ride' around his old tricycle, which had been

Key Questions

Careful questioning when exploring your child's dream can emphasize a particular subject area, such as making your own choices.

? Did it feel like this was your own special park?

? Why do you think dad and Sean were at the theme park?

? Could you have chosen to go on any ride you wanted?

? What was it like on the 'swooping' dipper ride?

abandoned in the garage. His father was delighted to help him and, using discarded boxes, rope and paints, they made it look like his very own ride. He had great fun playing on it in the garden with friends.

The fun fair was due in town soon and Eleanor asked if Steven would like to visit it with some friends when it arrived. Steven jumped at the chance to go even though Sean said that he was too old for fairs.

Dreamercise

Steven's dream provided an opportunity for the Superhero dreamercise (see page 125).

⏰ Eleanor asked Steven if he could have his dream again what would he do if he was a super hero? Steven replied that there would be a disaster on one of the rides and he would rescue people. Eleanor suggested he draw himself as a super hero.

⏰ At bedtime they looked at his drawings. 'Now,' said Eleanor, 'imagine you are back in your theme park. As you sleep you can be that super hero and tomorrow you can tell me about your adventures!' Steven laughed as he squirmed under the covers, anxious to start dreaming.

Queen of the Enchanted Wood

Gabriella's dream, aged nine

"*I found myself running through a beautiful wood with light streaming in between the branches. Everything sparkled as if it was made of precious stones. It was enchanted. Furry animals were running about, smiling and chattering about the Queen arriving. Then they all headed off towards a clearing. I ran after them and as I came to the clearing some of the animals shouted, 'The Queen! The Queen!' They were talking about me! I was in a flowing gown and my hair had amazingly grown all the way to the ground.*"

The Dream Context

Gabriella is an adopted child who lives with her loving adoptive parents and a much older sister, their biological child. She is confident, if a little quiet, and her adoptive parents have never had cause for concern, although they have often wished there was not such a large age gap between the two girls.

How Gabriella Felt

Gabriella conveyed a real sense of drama when recollecting her fantastical dream: Anna was surprised by her animated manner. The drama of the gems was balanced by the levity of the furry animals running about. She felt very happy in the dream, feeling very much part of the scene. Suddenly finding that she was the center of attention – the Queen – was very exciting. And she had what she had always wanted in waking life – long, flowing hair!

Critical Childhood Marker

Frequently when there is a large age gap between two children, each one feels and acts like an only child. Parents must be prepared to help the younger child through the essential stages of childhood in the same way as they did the older one.

Because they never have to learn to share with siblings close to their own age sometimes only children become a little self-centered. Parents sensitive to this issue ensure that their child realizes the importance of others' feelings and that the world does not revolve around them simply because they get more attention than most. 'Only' children can also seem grown up before their time. They are often quieter than children with near siblings, as they have not grown up in an environment where only the loudest voice is heard.

Aim of Analysis

From her answers to the key questions Anna felt reassured that this dream was truly a flight of fantasy and not a dream full of longing. For example, when talking about her hair in the dream, Gabriella said she thought such hair would be quite silly in real life. Anna planned to:

1 Help Gabriella feel confident enough to express her natural creativity.

2 Develop Gabriella's sense of drama based on the abundance of ideas in her dream.

3 Involve some friends in some play activity based on the dream.

Key Questions

Anna wanted to explore how much of the dream was pure fantasy and how much represented some sort of emotional longing.

? When you first came upon the beautiful wood what did you feel?

? Did the animals seem real to you?

? When you heard about the Queen, did you feel excited?

? What was it like finding out you were the Queen?

What Gabriella and Anna Did

Together they talked about Gabriella's dream and the creative scope it offered. Anna enjoyed their talk tremendously and Gabriella blossomed when allowed to talk about her creative potential.

Gabriella said she would like to write a story based on the dream. Anna asked, 'Why not write a short play?' Gabriella had never written a play and thought this was a great idea.

Gabriella was excited about drawing what she remembered from her dream. Anna suggested that she make a series of drawings that were like snapshots from different stages of her dream. They could then put these together to make a picture book. Anna gave Gabriella some gem-like glass

beads to decorate the cover of the book.

Anna suggested Gabriella invite some friends over to play dressing up. Gabriella wondered if her friends would act out her play. Anna suggested that she ask them to contribute their own ideas to the play to make it more of a shared activity. Gabriella felt there should be a queen in it but suggested they take turns playing that part. Anna was delighted.

RELATED THEMES

• **Jewels and Precious Metals** Depending on the emotion your child feels, these can represent a sense of drama or a sense of longing for something precious.

• **Friendly Animals** Your child is expressing a warm, creative nature.

• **Being Seen as a Grand Figure by Others** If accompanied by discomfort, your child may feel uncomfortable with praise or admiration. Alternatively, it may symbolize a desire to play a leading part.

• **Growth of a Body Part** Unusual growth in a dream can symbolize great pleasure, as with Gabriella's hair. However, if accompanied by anxiety, your child may feel things are moving, or growing, too quickly for them.

Psychedelic Shopping Spree

Jenny's dream, aged eleven

"I found myself in a weird shop full of crazy things. The woman who ran it insisted I have whatever I wanted for free, and pushed a cart into my hands. I was thrilled and started loading the cart with psychedelic clothes, shoes and gifts. They were wild colors and had gadgets attached to them. Then a noise from a huge gilded birdcage caught my attention. Inside were parrot-like birds of the most amazing colors. I couldn't hear exactly what they were saying but they were friendly, and somehow we seemed to understand each other!"

How Jenny Felt

Jenny thought her dream was fantastic. It had all the things she loves to have fun with – clothes, shoes and gadgets. She was in her own personal paradise and felt happy, even overwhelmed, throughout the dream. It had brought her fantasy of having a never-ending shopping spree to life. In addition to enjoying heaping things into her shopping cart, she thought that the talking birds were incredible. She woke up wishing she could have made her dream last longer.

The Dream Context

Jenny is a typical pre-teen. She has begun to experiment with her hair and clothes, and sometimes her parents disapprove of the look she creates. They do not want her worrying about her appearance and feel she is 'fashion mad'. Her mother, May Ling, remembers her own pre-teen years fondly – always running about in jeans – and she is frightened her daughter is growing up too quickly. However, on the whole May Ling feels that they have found the right balance between letting Jenny do more 'grown-up' things and restricting her behaviour.

Aim of Analysis

May Ling hoped that she and Jenny could find some common points of interest and develop some fun projects. She thought that:

1. Focusing on Jenny's dream would show her daughter that May Ling was interested in her inner world.
2. Together they could come up with some projects based on clothing from the dream.
3. She could encourage Jenny to do some creative writing.

What Jenny and May Ling Did

They had fun discussing the peculiar aspects of Jenny's dream.

Jenny decided she would keep a dream diary. May Ling thought this was a great idea and suggested she use her dreams as a basis for writing at school. Jenny had frequently complained that she was unable to think of any stories when the writing teacher set creative writing assignments. A dream diary would solve that problem (*see pages 128–9*).

May Ling was happy to watch the fun Jenny had in drawing and designing clothes based on the fashions in her dream. She asked if she could draw the gadgets too. Jenny replied that the dream had given her some ideas for exotic jewellery designs. Never before had she

Critical Childhood Marker

Little by little, as they grow up, children develop their own interests and learn how to make decisions for themselves. It is hard to know how much and when to relinquish parental control.

Pre-teens are usually keen to sever the emotional apron strings but do not have the knowledge or experience to weigh up situations accurately. They leap headfirst into something without considering the consequences. Suddenly they become interested in dressing in a particular way, or keeping certain company. While you need to protect your child's emotional wellbeing you also need to allow them to develop in their own direction.

expressed an interest in crafts. May Ling suggested they visit a crafts shop to buy a few things so that she could make some earrings or bracelets.

Jenny's little sister, Annie, admired her fashion drawings. They cut some out for Annie's paper dolls.

Key Questions

A wild dream gives you the chance to talk to your pre-teen about their natural creativity rather than arguing with them over boundaries concerning their behaviour.

? What first caught your attention?

? What was the sales woman like? (Here, substitute the person in your child's dream.)

? Describe the clothes and gadgets you saw? (Here, substitute the unusual objects in your child's dream.)

? Why do you think there were talking birds in your dream?

The Laughing Face in the Clouds

Jack's dream, aged four

"**I** was sitting high up in a tree in our back garden. The tree didn't have any branches. I was scared, as I couldn't hold on to anything. I saw some white, fluffy clouds appear in the sky. As I watched them I thought I saw something in them. I looked closely and it looked like a face. The big face started laughing. I tried to talk to the cloud face but it kept laughing. I started to cry. I never got down. "

Critical Childhood Marker

The 'three Ps' – Planning, Patience and a Positive attitude – are essential for successful toilet training. You need to plan where you put the training toilet – in a comfortable, warm and practical area. You need patience to say 'let's try again later' when your child has not wanted to sit on the potty. A positive attitude is required when your child has been dry for several days and then suddenly starts having accidents.

Children vary considerably in the speed with which they learn to use the toilet. Some are more in tune with their bodies than others and some are more easily distracted than others. External pressures can also affect a child's attitude to toilet or potty training.

How Jack Felt

Jack was extremely unsettled by his nightmare. He felt stranded up the tree and very alone. The absence of branches indicated how emotionally 'exposed' he felt. The clouds had intrigued Jack when they first appeared, but this feeling quickly turned to fear when he saw the big face, which he felt was laughing at him.

The Dream Context

Jack's mother, Diane, was worried about Jack's bed-wetting. Training him to use the toilet during the day had been easy – Jack had been happy to sit on the potty, keen to be a 'big boy' like his older brother Mark. Consequently, Jack had been dry during the day from the age of two. However, trying to get Jack out of diapers at night was proving difficult. Jack was constantly wetting the bed. Every evening at bedtime when Jack and Mark were in the bathroom cleaning their teeth, Diane would ask Jack to stand at the toilet. She would then leave the two boys for a few minutes before coming back to see if Jack had been successful.

Aim of Analysis

It was unusual for Jack to have nightmares and Diane was keen to find out how she could help Jack with whatever was bothering him. She wanted to:

1 Understand what was making Jack feel alone and laughed at.

2 Discover if it was related to his bed-wetting and help him to solve the problem.

3 Use the nightmare to develop positive communication with Jack.

What Jack and Diane Did

Jack told Diane that the unpleasant feeling aroused by the cloud laughing at him was the same as that caused by Mark when he made fun of him as he stood at the toilet. The lack of branches on Jack's tree symbolized how exposed and vulnerable he felt in Mark's presence. His mother had not realized that although Jack was trying to urinate he was so intimidated by Mark's teasing that he was going to bed with a full bladder and therefore wetting the bed during the night.

Diane understood that Jack needed privacy in the toilet. She asked Jack and his brother to use the bathroom one at a time.

To rebuild Jack's confidence Diane decided to wake him just before she went to bed to take him to the toilet, so preventing further wetting at night.

Key Questions

Diane wanted to find out why Jack felt alone and 'laughed at'. She couldn't think what had caused the nightmare unless it related to the bed-wetting.

? What did it feel like sitting in the tree? (Here, substitute the object your child was sitting in.)

? When you saw the fluffy, white clouds did you feel good?

? When the cloud face appeared and laughed did it remind you of anything or anyone?

? Why do you think you were alone in your nightmare?

Diane reassured Jack that he could tell her about any 'bad' feelings – there was no need to feel alone with his problems.

To boost Jack's confidence further, Diane made a great fuss of how fast he could run when the three of them next went to the park.

Diane asked Jack to draw a picture of the tree from his nightmare but to put lots of branches on it. Jack went a step further, drawing some colourful birds sitting on the branches.

Diane decided that Mark's teasing might indicate that he was feeling left out. She made a point of spending a few minutes talking to him every evening about the model he was constructing.

RELATED THEMES

• **Large Empty Spaces** Symbolize your child's sense of being alone. Do you need to encourage them to make friends or develop existing friendships?

• **Your Child Being Stared at or Observed** Your child may feel 'alone' while enduring unwanted attention. Perhaps they have been disciplined for something and now feel that people are watching their every move.

• **Missing Pieces** If your child dreams of something with crucial parts missing they may feel isolated.

Squashing the Intruder Ants

Jane's dream, aged seven

"I was dressed in my favorite party dress except it was pink instead of blue and I hate pink. That made me upset. I was in my room and the light was on because it was dark outside. There were ants coming in through the window. That made me angry as they didn't stop streaming in. I wanted to get rid of them, so I started squashing them with my shoe. It made me feel bad to find I enjoyed squashing them. I couldn't get rid of them and called to dad to help but he wouldn't come."

How Jane Felt

Although not a classic nightmare, Jane's dream left her feeling miserable. She was upset that her party dress was different and not to her liking. She was angry at the ant invasion of her room. This anger, coupled with her enjoyment of squashing the ants, gave Jane strong feelings of discomfort. Also, she felt great disappointment when her father 'wouldn't' come to help her get rid of the ants.

The Dream Context

Jane's mother died when she was three, and Jane treasures some photographs taken at her first three birthday parties in which her mom is by her side. Jane's father, Jacob, has been in a relationship with Shelley for ten months and last week set a date to marry her. For several months Jane has been jealous of Shelley, and recently has had angry outbursts for no apparent reason. Jacob is exasperated with Jane's behavior, unable to understand its cause.

Key Questions

Jacob wanted to understand the mix of emotions in Jane's nightmare. He thought the key to her recent behaviour might lie in the symbolism of the dream.

? Why do you think your dress was different? (Here, substitute the object that had changed in your child's dream.)

? Why do you think the ants were coming into your room?

? When you were squashing the ants were you reminded of any other feeling you've had?

? Why do you think I wouldn't come to you? (Here, substitute who wouldn't come when called in your child's dream.)

Dreamercise

Jacob used the Fairy-tale Ending dreamercise (see page 120) to encourage Jane to have happier dreams.

🕐 At bedtime Jacob asked Jane to repeat her ant story to him.

🕐 Then he asked her to think up a fairy-tale ending for it. Jane delighted in creating an extravagant but positive ending to her tale about the ants.

🕐 Jacob suggested that she could dream about the wonderful images that she had created.

🕐 Jane repeated the happy ending once more to him as she settled under the covers.

Aim of Analysis

Jacob used Jane's dream to try to encourage a better rapport between them. This included:

1	Learning how to communicate at a more meaningful level with Jane.
2	Discovering how to develop more positive feelings in Jane towards Shelley.
3	Encouraging Jane's creative side as an outlet for both negative and positive feelings.

What Jane and Jacob Did

Jacob was taken aback to find that the reason Jane felt he didn't come to 'help with the ants' was probably because he was with Shelley. He understood that firstly he must make Jane feel more secure. Her discomfiture about squashing the ants reflected Jane's contradictory feelings about Shelley. Jane liked her as a person but felt angry at the amount of attention she received from her father.

Jane associated party dresses with memories of her mother. That the dress in the dream was 'different' symbolized Jane's need to be reassured that her mother's place was not being taken. Since her mother's death, as time had passed, Jacob and Jane had visited her grave less frequently. Jacob decided to let Jane dictate the timing of the visits in future.

Jacob knew that the best time Jane had spent with Shelley was cycling. Jane loved her bike and Shelley liked the fresh air. He asked Jane if she would like to choose a destination for a cycling trip. Jane was excited about being allowed to choose.

Jacob asked Jane if she would make up a story about an ant family for him. Jane replied enthusiastically that she could also draw some pictures. The next time Shelley visited, Jacob made a big deal of showing her Jane's creative work. This gave Jane the chance to be center of attention.

Jacob made a point of including Jane in the day-to-day decisions. He wanted Jane to feel that she counted in the household.

Critical Childhood Marker

Children under the age of eight are naturally self-centered: their world is not based on emotional compromise yet. So, although the introduction of a baby or a new partner can signal the beginning of a rewarding period in the development of the parent-child relationship, at first the child may feel very threatened. To help your child adjust to the new circumstances, make them feel involved. Ask them how they feel about the situation. Find out what shared experiences they would like to have. Do not rush the new person into your child's life. And, most importantly, reassure your child of their importance in your world.

Trapped in a Rolling Ball

Adriana's dream, aged ten

"I was trapped inside a really big ball. I was wearing brightly colored clothes that looked really silly. I couldn't see out of the ball but I knew it was rolling. It was very frightening not knowing where it was going. It was cold inside the ball and really uncomfortable. No one seemed to hear me yelling. I gave up yelling and felt like crying. Then I thought I heard some voices. I listened really hard but couldn't make them out. I wanted to get home so badly."

How Adriana Felt

Adriana was really upset on waking after the nightmare, and had been unable to get back to sleep. She had felt consumed by the ball and completely out of control with the rolling motion. Not knowing where the ball was heading had been very frightening. Adriana did not usually express herself so emotionally and the strength of her feelings surprised Pelagia, who had not known how to comfort her.

The Dream Context

Adriana and her parents had recently moved to a new area because of her father's work. It had been Adriana's first move, and meant changing schools. Adriana had always been contented but not particularly adventurous or outgoing. Before the move her parents had been concerned that Adriana might have some difficulty settling in at her new school and had tried to make moving an exciting and positive prospect. However, during the busy days after the move they had largely forgotten their worries about Adriana.

Critical Childhood Marker

Moving house usually creates some anxiety in children. In general, the older the child, the more difficult it is for them to adapt, especially if they have been happily settled for a number of years and have developed strong friendships. Older children know how difficult it can be to break into an established group, whereas younger children are easily caught up in the excitement of choosing new bedroom furnishings and exploring the new neighbourhood. It is important that older children are able to discuss feelings of unhappiness or loneliness with their parents, who will need to help them adjust to their new surroundings and circumstances.

Aim of Analysis

It became clear from talking about the nightmare that Adriana had found the move very difficult. Pelagia wanted to explore a number of issues:

1 The silly clothes indicated that Adriana felt she really stood out. Pelagia therefore thought it was important to think of ways to get Adriana to blend in.

2 She wished to find out how Adriana felt about inviting new friends over after school.

3 She wanted to find ways of building Adriana's confidence in herself.

What Adriana and Pelagia Did

Her overwhelming fearfulness in the nightmare reminded Adriana of the feeling she had each day as she entered her new school. Pelagia thought that if she could help Adriana become more confident in herself, she would find making new relationships at school easier. This in turn would help her to feel more in control and less frightened in her new environment. She also felt it was important to develop a deeper relationship with Adriana.

Pelagia encouraged Adriana to join some school clubs to enable her to get to know some other children with similar interests. Adriana decided to join the drama and history clubs.

Pelagia thought Adriana's approaching birthday would be the ideal opportunity to invite several children over. Adriana said she wanted to make one

Key Questions

Pelagia wanted to see if Adriana's nightmare held a particular message for her as a parent. Could something be learned from it about her daughter's deeper feelings?

? What was the first thing you remember about finding yourself in the ball?

? What was the strongest feeling you had while trapped in the ball?

? Have you felt this before?

? Who do you think was talking and why do you think they couldn't hear you?

good friend and suggested inviting just one new acquaintance.

Pelagia and Adriana joked about the strange clothes from the nightmare. Could they be used as a basis for costume ideas for a school play, Pelagia wondered. Adriana leapt at the suggestion of doing some costume drawings. When her father arrived home from work Adriana proudly showed off her sketches and excitedly told him about her various plans.

Her parents agreed that seeing her old friends would give Adriana a boost, so they suggested visiting their old town soon. Adriana was thrilled and immediately phoned her old friends to plan a get together.

RELATED THEMES

• **Out-of-control Car or Vehicle**
Your child needs help getting on top of their negative feelings.

• **Trapped Inside a Container**
Your child feels unable to express themselves.

• **Wearing Silly Clothes with People Watching** Your child is worried that they are showing feelings they want to keep private.

Attacked by Giant Plants

Jason's dream, aged nine

"I was racing through our garden as plants lashed out at my ankles. I tried to go faster and faster but they grew longer. One wrapped around my leg but I managed to keep pulling myself along. I knew they were out to get me. My heart was pounding and I felt I was going to die if I didn't get out of the garden. As I finally reached the bottom of the garden, our wooden gate became the school gate. It was made of glistening metal and grew taller and taller so I couldn't reach the latch."

82

How Jason Felt

Jason's nightmare left him paralysed with fear. He could not understand why he dreamt of monstrous, terrifying plants. He recalled feeling angry when he reached the garden gate and it turned into the schoolyard gate, trapping him in the evil garden. His mother, Elizabeth, had heard him crying out in his sleep and had come to comfort him. Even so, it had taken him the rest of the night to shake off his fear.

The Dream Context

Jason was quite a small boy who was being subjected to bullying at school. Jason wanted to tell his mother and grandfather but he was frightened that if he did so, and it got back to the bullies, they would bully him more. At the moment the bullying took the form of name calling, prodding, pushing and threats. However, Jason was scared that the bullies would carry out their threat to 'beat him up' if he did not bring them more of his lunch money soon.

Key Questions

Jason's mother asked her father who lived with them, if he would talk to Jason about the nightmare. Jason and his grandfather, Art, had a close relationship and Elizabeth felt that Jason might be more willing to talk to him about his fears.

? What made you think it was our garden? Were you alone?

? Were the plants like people in any way? (Here, substitute the object that became lifelike in your child's dream.

? How did you manage to keep going when the plant grabbed you?

? Why did you think your fear turned to anger at the school gate?

83

Critical Childhood Marker

Bullying is a particularly destructive experience that strikes at the heart of a child. They question why they were singled out and begin to believe that it is because they are not good enough. If bullying goes unchecked they can lose all self-esteem and come to believe that they 'deserve' it.

Successfully meeting such a challenge can work wonders for the child's self-confidence and ability to handle future problems. The problem-solving skills required include being able to express their distress, learning to assert themselves, managing peer pressure and developing strategies to deflect unwanted attention and building self-confidence. If the problem is not resolved, a long-lasting sense of failure and an inability to cope may result.

Aim of Analysis

Art used the nightmare to meet a number of objectives:

1. To gain a deeper understanding of the anxiety at the heart of it.
2. To develop Jason's confidence within the family and in handling social problems.
3. To encourage Jason to take up an activity that would develop his social skills.

What Jason and Art Did

It soon became apparent to his grandfather that the nightmare related to the bullying Jason was experiencing but had kept secret. It was obvious from his answers to the key questions that Jason was very angry that none of the teachers had noticed the bullying. Clearly he felt that it was OK if a teacher had realized what was going on but not for Jason to have told them.

Art assured Jason that it was best to inform the school of the problem. If he did so, Jason wanted to be sure that the school would not name him to the bullies. They decided to contact Jason's favorite teacher first.

Art asked Jason if he would like his older cousin to keep an eye on him at school. Jason thought this was a good idea as his cousin was two years older than him and one year older than the bullies. That the nightmare was located in their own garden indicated how much Jason wanted to be able to solve the problem himself, or with the help of his family.

Jason joined the boy scouts and within weeks was taking great pleasure in the various pursuits available. He was obviously learning a lot about himself and others, and Art and Elizabeth were pleased with the positive changes they noticed in him.

Jason practised making assertive statements with Art.

Art asked Jason to make a drawing of his tormentors. Jason had great fun ripping up his drawings. His attitude to the bullies was 'take that!'

Dreamercise

Jason was feeling more positive by bedtime, so Art suggested trying the Bash the Baddy dreamercise (see page 124).

Art asked Jason to visualize himself as bigger than the bullies. Jason said he could imagine himself as a great big giant. Art replied, 'Then you will be a giant in your next dream.'

Art asked what he would do as a giant. Jason said he would bounce the bullies along by the toes of his boots until they begged him to stop! He would decide when they had been punished enough.

'And what about the monster plants?' Art asked. 'I would be so huge that I'd pull them out and tear them up. They'll never scare me again,' replied Jason.

Searching in the Dark for a Lost Pet

Zoe's dream, aged six

"I was looking out of my window. It was dark outside but I thought I saw my dog Tiko run across the paving stones. I jumped out of my window to get him. I was really scared but I wanted him back. I ran where I thought he'd gone but couldn't see him. I felt very upset to be outside in the dark on my own. Then I thought I heard Tiko rustling in some bushes. I chased the noise, crying out his name but no sound came from my voice. As I ran I tripped and slipped down a black tunnel. I kept slipping and tumbling until I woke up. "

How Zoe Felt

Zoe described a range of disturbing emotions in her nightmare. Looking out of the window into the dark, Zoe had felt lonely. Her excitement rose when she thought Tiko might be out there. But this was quickly replaced with fear when she realized she was alone in the dark. No sound came from her voice, symbolizing that she was not being 'listened to'. Running and then tumbling down the tunnel created even more anxiety and a feeling of being completely alone in a terrifying experience.

Critical Childhood Marker

Children under four often appear quite blasé about bereavement. Usually they are more unsettled by the sight of others grieving than by the thought that they will never see a treasured pet or relative again. Children over four have a more developed understanding of time and what it might mean that someone is 'never coming back': they feel bereavement deeply. Losing a pet is frequently a child's first experience of death. It can lead them to discover a lot about their emotions, and how to handle being sad or angry.

The Dream Context

Zoe's pet dog, Tiko, had died of natural causes two days before the nightmare. Zoe had cherished Tiko. She had helped her father feed him, groom him and walk him. Tiko could be found curled up on her bed every evening as she went to sleep. Zoe had been devastated when Tiko became ill. The vet found a congenital heart problem and said she was surprised that Tiko had managed to live for almost two years. This had been of no comfort to Zoe who had also been unimpressed by her father's promise to get her another dog. Zoe wanted Tiko back.

Aim of Analysis

As the nightmare centred on Zoe's sense that Tiko was in the garden, her father, Charles, understood that it was about her grief. Charles wanted to use the nightmare to help her handle her grief.

1 Talking about the nightmare would allow them to talk about Tiko, which they had not done since his death.

2 Exploring Zoe's strong feelings would help her to gain control of them.

3 Something positive, like hope, might come out of this. Specifically, they might discover how Zoe would like to commemorate Tiko's life.

Key Questions

Her father was surprised that Zoe had felt so very alone. Careful questioning would help him explore this.

? Did you feel hopeful when looking out of the window? (Here, substitute whatever your child was gazing through or at.)

? Did you feel that Tiko was lost outside?

? When you felt scared was there anything that could have made it better?

? Did the feeling of falling down the tunnel remind you of anything? (Here, substitute what your child fell into.)

What Zoe and Charles Did

Charles found that talking to Zoe about her nightmare opened up communication between the two of them. As he was separated from Zoe's mother and Tiko had been a shared joy for Zoe and him, it brought a special closeness to their conversation.

Zoe's fear seemed to be partly to do with not knowing where Tiko had gone. Charles asked Zoe to imagine a special place where dogs go to once they have died. Zoe said she hoped Tiko was living in a never-ending field filled with flowers and sunshine.

Charles suggested that Zoe draw a picture of this lovely place. Her drawing reinforced what a happy life Tiko had had with her, and commemorated Zoe's love for her pet.

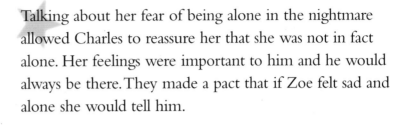

Talking about her fear of being alone in the nightmare allowed Charles to reassure her that she was not in fact alone. Her feelings were important to him and he would always be there. They made a pact that if Zoe felt sad and alone she would tell him.

Charles had put away Tiko's food and water bowls, and his toys, thinking they would upset Zoe. Zoe asked if they could put them out again for now. Zoe felt that by putting his things away her father was trying to forget Tiko, something that she never wanted to do.

RELATED THEMES

Nightmares are common after a bereavement. They throw up troubling emotions which your child may not be able to put into words.

• **Losing a Pet or a Person** Sense of loss is often symbolized in a dream by being separated from the dead pet or person. Usually this is accompanied by feelings of anxiety. Your child may need reassurance from you that no one else is going to be 'lost'.

• **The Dead Pet or Person Cannot 'See' your Child** This may indicate unfinished business. Your child has not been allowed to say their goodbyes in the way they would like to. Ask them how they would like to commemorate their pet or family member.

A Vast Treacherous Staircase

Andrew's dream, aged eleven

"We were playing in an empty grey old building. One of the guys yelled to the rest of us to come upstairs. We all ran over and the children in front of me started racing up the stairs. It looked like the staircase would collapse and I felt frightened. I tried to grab the rail but my hand slipped off. I wanted to climb the stairs but I didn't seem to have the strength. One boy shouted from the top, 'He didn't want to come up anyway!' It was awful."

The Dream Context

Andrew had never found school easy. His parents were aware that even his best sometimes fell a bit short but they tended not to push him. Recently, schoolwork had taken on more depth and Andrew was really falling behind. He had not mentioned this to his parents as he was unsure how to express his fears and feelings of inadequacy. He was dreading his parents' reaction to his next school report.

Critical Childhood Marker

At school the pressure to provide detailed subject reports, complete comprehensive exercises and participate in more complex discussions begins around the age of eleven. Many children flourish at this point but some find the challenge daunting.

Parents should try not to lose sight of the way the syllabus changes from year to year. Supporting their child as they tackle the earlier hurdles of reading and basic maths can boost their confidence enough to continue well. Ensuring that they have adequate study facilities, or extra encouragement or tuition if necessary, also helps.

How Andrew Felt

As the dream began, Andrew felt a little apprehensive about being in a strange, dilapidated building. However, he was caught up in the general excitement when they headed for the staircase to join the boy on the top floor. After that the dream took on a nightmarish quality for Andrew, who felt he could not climb the staircase like the other children, no matter how hard he tried.

Aim of Analysis

Andrew's mother, Rose, thought this was the perfect chance to talk to her youngest son about his feelings – something they didn't do very often. She wished to:

1. Identify any problem Andrew might be experiencing.

2. Build Andrew's confidence about school and promote Andrew's positive qualities.

3. Find out if Andrew needed some sort of professional help.

What Andrew and Rose Did

Andrew surprised Rose when they talked about his nightmare. He seemed to be able to express the feelings it evoked very well: it was as if a floodgate had been opened. Once she realized that the nightmare related to his feelings about schoolwork, Rose felt confident they could do something about the problem.

Andrew talked openly about his fear of failing at school. Rose suggested they talk to his favorite teacher about what action they could take.

Andrew's best subject was geography. Rose suggested applying his geographical knowledge to other subjects. Andrew suggested that for creative writing he could base his story on the characters' surroundings. When writing an essay on a famous battle he could focus on how the geography of the site helped determine the outcome.

Dreamercise

Rose suggested trying the 'control panel' dreamercise (see page 123).

🕐 *TAKE CONTROL* As he headed for bed, Rose asked Andrew how he would take control of a nightmare. Andrew said he would force himself to do what the others were doing.

🕐 *VISUALIZE* Rose asked him to replay the nightmare but to visualize himself racing ahead and beating the others up the staircase.

🕐 *CONTROL THE FEAR* Andrew was to say 'No, I can do it!' if the paralyzing fear returned during a nightmare.

Key Questions

Not knowing what this nightmare was about led Andrew's mother to explore it thoroughly.

? Did the building look familiar in any way?

? Were the children friends from school?

? What did you think about the boy who was leading the others upstairs?

? Did you wish you could be first?

? When you couldn't get up the stairs was the feeling familiar to you?

Andrew was concerned that other students should not know of his struggles. His teacher set up some extra tutoring discreetly to improve skills such as note taking.

Andrew felt relieved that his struggle was now out in the open. Rose felt closer to him and decided to have a regular 'special' time with him to monitor his feelings. Periodically, she reminded him how positive it felt to share his concerns, and asked him to continue to believe in himself.

Rose encouraged Andrew to go on the school's geography field trip. Previously he had declined the chance but with his new-found confidence he was excited about participating.

Searching for Lost Comfort

Chloe's dream, aged eight

"I was panicking, searching for my favorite red jumper. I found all my other clothes but not that jumper. I felt like I'd die if I didn't find it. I opened a dresser drawer – inside were some bug-like creatures. I slammed it shut. I was scared and called to my mother. She didn't reply. I started searching again. 'It must be here somewhere!' I shouted. Then I broke down crying, feeling completely lost in my own room."

The Dream Context

Chloe's parents have recently divorced. Her father, Chris, has moved to a small flat a few miles away, although recently he has been considering moving further away because of his work. This has panicked Chloe, who is frightened that the father she is very fond of will abandon her. Chloe has not spoken to her mom, Janet, about her fears because her mom never has anything good to say about Chris. Chloe loves her father but does not know what to do to show him how much she wants him to stay nearby.

Critical Childhood Marker

Children often experience emotional problems once their parents' divorce is finalized because of an inability to deal with the emotional vacuum that is left after the tensions of the divorce process have gone. Children over seven can find it very difficult to adjust, filling the void with a fear of abandonment and depression about being unable to 'do' anything to help the situation.

If either parent has used their child as an emotional crutch or as part of a power struggle with their 'ex', the child comes to see their role more as healer than innocent party. They then fear that if they do not always play a particular role with each parent they may be rejected.

How Chloe Felt

Chloe was clearly frightened when she called out to her mother in the middle of the night. The nightmare had started with a sense of desperation over the lost jumper – Chloe felt unable to cope unless she found her favourite item of clothing. Opening the drawer to find bugs was almost too much to bear. Slamming the drawer shut did not rid her of her fear, so she called to her mother. When no help arrived she felt unable to cope and completely broke down.

Aim of Analysis

The nightmare gave Janet insight into how Chloe felt about her parents and the divorce. Janet wanted to:

1. Use the conversation about the nightmare to develop better communication with Chloe.
2. Use the nightmare as a basis for talking to Chris about Chloe's fears.
3. Help Chloe devise some coping strategies to overcome fears in the future.
4. Handle her own feelings more carefully so that Chloe would not be affected by them.

What Chloe and Janet Did

The analysis of the nightmare revealed how frightened Chloe was of losing her father. She wondered why, if she was a 'good' daughter, he would want to move away. Chloe felt that Janet had not come to her in her nightmare when she called because she had not actually made any noise, symbolizing how frightened she was of telling her mother about her fear.

Janet and Chloe made a pact: Chloe could ask her mother any questions and she would do her best to answer them. Once a week, Janet determined to do a 'Chloe check', to see if there was anything Chloe was uncomfortable with. She did not want her to slam the drawer on her uncomfortable emotions (the bugs in her nightmare).

Janet decided that her own feelings about the divorce should not prevent Chris from being involved when

Chloe had doubts or fears. The familiar old jumper Chloe was so frightened she had lost symbolized the comfort she was afraid of losing from her father. Janet discussed the nightmare with Chris. He decided to reconsider the need to move and to discuss it with Chloe only if he was certain he would be moving.

Janet got to know another divorced mother nearby and invited her two children to play with Chloe. Janet introduced Chloe to a 'take control' strategy: if Chloe felt worried she was to visualize her favourite cartoon character in the midst of her usual antics and throw her own cares to the wind. They also practised positive affirmations, such as: 'I'm in charge of my feelings. I won't let things get on top of me! I can talk to mom or dad.'

Key Questions

Chloe's nightmare worried Janet, who wanted to understand the disturbing symbolism.

? Why did you feel you needed the red jumper? (Here, substitute the item your child was searching for.)

? Did your panic over the jumper remind you of anything in waking life?

? What did you feel when you saw the bug-like creatures?

? Were you angry when I didn't answer you?

Pots and Pans Rain Down

Derek's dream, aged eleven

"I was looking around a kitchen, although I wasn't sure it was ours. I pulled on the handles of a large cupboard. The doors flew open and a whole load of pots and pans came tumbling out. I felt terrible. I quickly started to pick them up but they fell to pieces in my hands. I had a rising sense of dread that I'd never get the mess cleared up. I thought I heard my father's voice, although I don't think he knew what was going on and I wasn't sure it was him."

98

The Dream Context

Derek's parents had high expectations of their eldest son. He was constantly reminded by his father of how lucky he was to be heading for college. His father, Lawrence, had wanted to be a lawyer but had had to leave school early as his family could no longer support him financially. Derek dreaded it when the conversation turned to his future, feeling angry at the weight on his shoulders. His parents assumed he was happy to have opportunities that they had not had. Derek was becoming increasingly withdrawn.

How Derek Felt

Derek described a mixture of emotions in his nightmare. The trepidation he felt at not knowing whether it was his kitchen was replaced by the desire to open the cupboard. Much to his dismay, opening the cupboard created a problem he could not cope with: all the pots and pans spilled out. When they fell apart in his hands he felt guilty, as though it were his responsibility, and fearful, because he could not fix them. His father was a shadowy figure in the background who made him feel uncomfortable.

Critical Childhood Marker

Many parents fail to recognize the effect on their child when they try to live their own dreams through their child. It is critical to a child's self-esteem to feel loved and nurtured for the individual they are and not for the potential they offer for fulfilling their parents' lives. Older children are particularly vulnerable. Of course, parents must encourage their children to do their best. What they must guard against is trying to mould their children's interests and overall direction to suit their own unfulfilled dreams. Listen to your child. Find out what interests them and encourage those interests. They may not become the doctor you wish you had been but they will be happier individuals if nurtured for themselves.

Aim of Analysis

Helen and Lawrence realized that they had not allowed Derek to express himself around them. This had led to feelings that he was not good enough to meet their high expectations. They wanted to:

1 Stop talking about their expectations for Derek and to build a more positive relationship with him by focusing on his hopes and desires.

2 Enable Derek to join in some activities that he would enjoy.

3 Demonstrate to Derek that he counted just the way he was with some simple confidence-boosting exercises.

What Derek and his Parents Did

Feeling unable to cope with the situation in his nightmare clearly reflected Derek's waking feelings. The shadowy image of his father symbolized how he was ever-present in his thoughts. Derek felt obliged to do what his father wanted. This concerned both his parents who truly wanted his happiness.

Within weeks of their agreement not to talk about Derek's future, he seemed happier in himself.

When encouraged to start getting more involved with activities of his choice, Derek joined the French club at school. They had no idea he enjoyed French. Derek explained he loved the food tasting in the French class – perhaps they had a budding chef?

Key Questions

Both Derek's parents wanted to discuss his nightmare with him. They hoped their questions might lead them to understand the meaning behind this unusual nightmare.

? Did you recognize anything in the kitchen?

? Why did you want to look in the cupboard?

? What did it feel like pulling on the handles?

? What did you think when the pots fell apart?

? Did you want to find your father?

Helen and Lawrence made a point of asking Derek's opinion on matters concerning the whole family. They gave him time to answer and lots of positive feedback. Lawrence asked Derek for his help with jobs around the house – something he had never done before. Helen made a point of asking Derek about his preferences on everyday things: What would he like for Sunday lunch? What video should they take out? Where would he like the family camping holiday to be? They were not very surprised when he suggested France.

RELATED THEMES

- **Not being Able to Open a Door** Your child may feel frustrated in something they are trying to do or being required to do.

- **Objects Tumbling on to your Child** If they feel unable to do anything about this, they may feel overwhelmed by something in their life.

- **Things Breaking Apart when Touched** Your child may be experiencing very low self-esteem. Quite literally they do not trust their own 'touch' not to damage something.

- **Panic or Discomfort at the Sound of a Voice** Whose voice worries them in their dream? They may feel unsure of their standing with that person.

The Wrong Face on the Doll

Samantha's dream, aged nine

"I was playing with my doll with the fashion wardrobe. Some of my friends were in the playroom playing with other toys. I was making my doll walk to the shops. Suddenly her head fell off. When I picked it up to put back on the doll's body, I was upset because it wasn't my doll's face on the head. It was Jane's face! I started to get angry about it. I wanted my own doll's face back. I looked over to my other friends. I wanted to see if Jane was in the group because I wanted to tell her what I thought of this."

How Samantha Felt

Samantha's dream represented the conflict she felt with Jane – a recent arrival to her group of friends. Although initially friends, Samantha had come to see Jane as a threat. Samantha was angry and wanted to tell Jane what she thought of her but she was not 'there' to tell, indicating that she felt that Jane did not really listen to her. That her other friends were simply playing in the background revealed Samantha's contentment with the group as a whole.

The Dream Context

Samantha has always been a fairly assertive young girl and has always been able to persuade other children without bullying them. A couple of weeks ago, a new girl – Jane – joined her class at school. At first Samantha talked excitedly about her new friend – another assertive girl. More recently Samantha had complained that Jane was trying to take her friends away and they had an argument over what game to play.

Key Questions

Pat wanted to explore the feelings brought to the fore by Samantha's dream.

? What did you feel when you were first playing?

? What was your strongest feeling when your doll's face became Jane's? (Here, substitute when your child dreams of someone's face in an unusual way.)

? Why do you think that happened?

? Was everything else OK in your dream?

103

Critical Childhood Marker

As children grow socially more independent of their family, friendships, and difficulties with them, take on greater significance. If your child faces difficulties in a particular friendship let them know you are there if they need help or advice but try not to interfere too much. If your child chooses to discuss a problem, then listen. Guide them in finding their own solutions. Boost their confidence in their ability to determine what is right and wrong in the way they treat their friends.

Aim of Analysis

Pat knew that sometimes arguments between children could spiral out of control and she did not want Samantha to develop a feud with Jane. Pat determined to:

1 Help Samantha develop ways to overcome arguments.

2 Ensure that Samantha felt confident socially so that she would not find the natural assertiveness of others threatening.

3 Encourage Samantha to make up with and play with Jane.

What Samantha and Pat Did

Pat felt that the best starting point was a quiet discussion with Samantha about friendships.

Pat asked Samantha if her old friends still played with her. Samantha took some comfort from the fact that they did. They then discussed how small incidents could be blown out of proportion. Did the argument she had had with Jane really mean anything? Samantha obviously felt challenged by it.

Pat bolstered Samantha's confidence in communicating by practicing the 'what you might say' game using role play. Pat pretended to be Barbie and said something provocative but funny, such as: 'You have to be Barbie's little sister!' Samantha had to reply, giving two reasons why she should be nothing of the sort. Samantha was soon communicating her thoughts without being argumentative.

Dreamercise

....

As Samantha was quite artistic, Pat decided to try the Dream Pathways dreamercise (*see page 122*).

🕐 One evening Pat asked Samantha to draw a scene in which two girls were playing happily together. Pat explained that the scene should represent a place that Samantha would like to visit, perhaps in a dream. Samantha drew a beautiful and bold scene in which two girls were running through a sparkling fountain in the sunshine.

🕐 'How do you find the pathway there?' Pat asked. 'By smelling the beautiful flowers,' Samantha replied. Later, as Pat tucked her into bed, she asked Samantha to close her eyes, count to ten and she would find herself at the dream pathway. 'Now you will visit your lovely garden with a friend,' Pat said softly.

Pat suggested that Samantha invite Jane over. Samantha suggested they bake a chocolate cake together. When the day arrived Pat asked the girls to take turns placing the ingredients into the mixing bowl. They shared well and talked excitedly about how to ice the cake.

Pat suggested that for her next creative writing assignment she could write about two girls who argued terribly. Samantha said that one of them could have a crash on her bicycle and the other could come to her rescue. She said she would write a happy ending in which they became firm friends.

Singled Out by a Teacher

Tiffany's dream, aged ten

"I was in the maths classroom and everything seemed really dreary. It was freezing cold and I felt uncomfortable. As I reached for my sweater, the teacher yelled at me: 'Come here!' I walked up to the front of the class with my hands clasped over my face as if to hide my face. Suddenly the teacher said, 'It's game time!' He grabbed my hands and started spinning me around. The whole class stared. I tried to yell but my hands still seemed to be on my face. No one came to stop him. **"**

106

How Tiffany Felt

Her nightmare began with a dismal, resigned feeling, which turned into dread when the teacher called her up to the front. She tried to hide by covering her face. Even though she felt this might anger her teacher more she could not remove her hands. Her worst fears were realized when he made fun of her, turning her into a 'game' for the class.

The Dream Context

Tiffany felt very undermined by her maths teacher who often made her feel small and sometimes embarrassed her by singling her out in class. She had never discussed his behavior with her mother, Nancy, or stepfather, Steve, as she was often unsure of exactly what he did. Tiffany had always been an average student and they were surprised when her maths grade was much lower than usual.

Critical Childhood Marker

A child's scholastic and personal development can be affected quite markedly by individual teachers. A positive, enthusiastic teacher can motivate your child to learn, while a negative, thoughtless teacher can severely damage your child's self-esteem and dampen their interest in learning.

If parents are aware of any difficulties with a particular teacher, they can bolster their child against any negative consequences. Older children would rather know that their parents understand the difficulties they face, and offer them support and comfort at home, than visit the school to discuss any problems with a teacher.

Aim of Analysis

Nancy was concerned that Tiffany's negative experience with the teacher would undermine her whole self-confidence. The fact that Tiffany felt no one in the class 'paid attention' to her plight revealed a potential threat to her self-esteem. Nancy wanted to:

1. Find out if the problem was so serious a meeting should be arranged with the teacher.
2. Develop assertiveness skills that Tiffany could use with the teacher.
3. Encourage Tiffany to discuss problems at school with them.
4. Determine if the unhappiness had undermined her maths learning and whether she would need some help catching up.

What Tiffany and her Parents Did

Nancy and Steve felt hurt and angry that their daughter seemed to be singled out and thought a meeting with the maths teacher was important.

Tiffany was against her parents seeing the teacher. She was sure it would worsen the situation. They agreed that if matters did not improve they could visit the teacher at a later date.

Nancy and Steve wanted to build Tiffany's confidence. They made a point of telling her how much they appreciated her help with her younger sister, and asked her to take charge of planning her sister's eighth birthday party.

Key Questions

Nancy wanted to understand Tiffany's unhappiness.

? Did you feel alone or part of the class?

? Why do you think you tried to hide your face? (Here, substitute whatever your child tried to hide about themselves.)

? When you were being spun around what were you thinking?

? Was it the real math teacher?

108

Nancy and Steve asked Tiffany what her teacher did to undermine her. She listed about four things. Top of the list was being put on the spot with difficult questions, which made her tongue-tied and caused the teacher to remark on her lack of attention. When asked what she thought was a better response, she said: 'I don't know the answer to that.' They praised her straightforwardness. They worked through all the problem areas and practised the responses that Tiffany herself suggested.

Steve bought some entertaining maths exercise books and set aside some time each weekend to work through them with Tiffany. They had a big bag of treats on hand to munch on.

RELATED THEMES

• **Being Singled Out in Class** Your child feels threatened, unless of course they do something marvellous in front of their class.

• **The Teacher Ignoring Them** Your child may feel excluded in this particular class.

• **Alone in their Classroom** Your child may feel lonely at school or they may feel left behind in their school work.

• **Looking into a Classroom** They may feel excluded if the image is accompanied by anxious or miserable feelings.

The Man at the End of the Bed

Alex's dream, aged eight

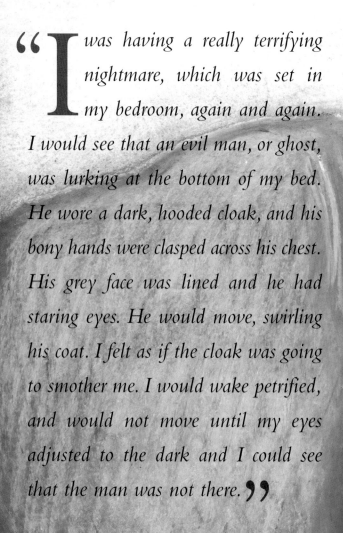

"I was having a really terrifying nightmare, which was set in my bedroom, again and again. I would see that an evil man, or ghost, was lurking at the bottom of my bed. He wore a dark, hooded cloak, and his bony hands were clasped across his chest. His grey face was lined and he had staring eyes. He would move, swirling his coat. I felt as if the cloak was going to smother me. I would wake petrified, and would not move until my eyes adjusted to the dark and I could see that the man was not there."

110

The Dream Context

Alex's parents were in the middle of an acrimonious separation. Vicious arguments would erupt between his mother and father. Alex's mother, Sarah, saw that he was deeply affected by these, but she did not know how to talk about his feelings. Alex's father, John, took the view that Alex was old enough to understand that divorcing parents inevitably argue. Alex was living with a mother who felt ineffectual and a father who was in denial.

Key Questions

As with any nightmare, settling the child is the perogative. This can take the form of validating the child's fear with statements like, 'Oh, that does sound very frightening', followed by reassuring statements such as, 'I'm here now, nothing can happen to you'. The next morning Sarah asked in calm tones:

? What was this awful man like? Sarah took note of the fearful, smothering cloak.

? Did you feel trapped, as if you could not move? It is important to explore a child's feelings if they have remained stationary in a nightmare.

? Did the way you felt in your nightmare remind you of any feelings you have had when awake?

Aim of Analysis

To try to understand a nightmare will help you understand your child's fears and anxieties:

1 Explore the sorts of feelings arising in the nightmare. Does your child show fear and anxiety? Are they hopeless? Are they angry? These will point to the meaning.

2 Think about new ways your child may be able to express themselves.

3 Enable the child to gain control of the part of their life responsible for their negative feelings.

What Alex and Sarah Did

With discussion Sarah found that Alex was feeling trapped by the arguments. Alex recounted how the feeling when the phantom was there, was the same feeling he had when the arguing began. If he runs from bed during the nightmare the man will swoop, if he stays still so will the man. This is how he feels about the arguing. If he makes a fuss he is frightened his angry parents will turn on him, so instead he 'freezes' and suffers in silence.

Suggest your child draws a picture of the evil 'phantom'. Then ask them to scribble out the drawing aggressively or even rip it up. Action is particularly important when they are inactive in the nightmare. Tell them, 'See, you are stronger than they are!'

The *Key Questions* opened lines of communication for Alex and Sarah. Sarah asked Alex if he'd like to have

Dreamercise

The nightmare preventer:

🕐 *Repeat their strong 'control' chant with them before bedtime.*

🕐 *Ask what they would like to dream about perhaps try the Adventurous Journey dreamercise (see page 121). Have them fill in some detail.*

🕐 *Suggest they imagine an invisible force field around their bedroom. No one can get in except mum and dad!*

regular family chats to be updated about the divorce. Alex said yes, and was reassured that he could always ask.

With recurrent nightmares it is good to practice 'control' statements during the day. What does your child want to say to the bad man? Things like, 'I'm stronger than you, you don't even exist, and you can't come back!' are good. You can make a chant of these (giggling while you create a chant is good!). Get them to shake their fists and repeat the chant in a commanding tone.

Critical Childhood Marker

Divorce and separation present particular problems for each age group. Eight to ten year-olds may understand about relationships – some just fail to work out. However, they are still emotionally volatile like younger children, and their emotions frequently dominate their rational thoughts. This age is prone to feelings of guilt – that they are the cause of their parents' divorce because they are still highly egocentric. They believe life's situations, and most explanations, involve them. Much reassurance is needed that they are not to blame.

Trapped like a Wild Animal

Marco's dream, aged seven

"I was thrashing around, desperate to escape from something that seemed to hold me. I felt trapped like a wild animal. There were some tall shapes, like shadows, above me but I couldn't make out who they were. I was angry with them because they wouldn't help me. As I struggled I saw a building in front of me. I wanted to get there but no matter how hard I tried I couldn't move from where I was. The tall shapes seemed to loom over me. I kicked out with my feet and they disappeared. I was all alone and that was worse."

How Marco Felt

At the beginning of Marco's nightmare he felt out of control, thrashing about without even being sure why. Marco felt something beyond his control was holding him back. This turned to anger when the shadowy shapes around him did not communicate with him. The worst part of the nightmare was his feeling of isolation at the end. His mother thought he was describing feelings of rejection.

The Dream Context

Marco was a handful at the best of times. His behavior went beyond boisterous. His mother, Sylvia, did not know how to cope with his increasingly aggressive behavior, and did not dare leave him alone for even a few minutes with his little brother in case he lost his temper with him. She also worried that Marco did not seem to have any friends, at least none visited from school, and Marco never seemed to be invited anywhere. One time he complained to his mother that he thought no one liked him.

Key Questions

If your child is describing something very painful to them it is important to be sensitive in your questioning. Sylvia was aware that the nightmare left Marco feeling very unhappy.

? What wild animal did you feel like?

? Who do you think the shapes were? Mum and Dad?

? Why did you want to get to the building? Was it safe there?

? What sort of building was it?

Aim of Analysis

By listening to Marco's answers to the key questions, Sylvia felt sure the nightmare related to his aggressive impulses. Marco described the building as 'secure' – he would be safe if he could get there. But the shadows prevented him from reaching it, making him angry. Sylvia decided that:

1	It was time to get to the bottom of Marco's aggressive behavior.
2	Marco needed to learn how to handle frustration and anger.
3	Marco needed to believe his parents were behind him.
4	They should encourage activities that would use some of his natural energy.

What Marco and Sylvia Did

Marco's father worked away from home and Sylvia felt a bit overwhelmed looking after two young boys. However, she was determined to help him control his aggressive impulses.

Sylvia consulted with the school, which was very supportive once they realized that she was essentially coping on her own. One teacher suggested that perhaps Marco missed his father. Sylvia had noticed that Marco behaved less aggressively around his father. Sylvia asked her husband to telephone more frequently and to send postcards to Marco. Marco loved receiving these.

Critical Childhood Marker

Some children find it difficult to monitor their own aggressive impulses. One moment they are playing happily, the next they are lashing out at someone who has upset them. Left unchecked, aggressive behavior can cause them to be shunned by their peers, resulting in feelings of rejection and then more anger. The child may become depressed because of their feeling of being out of control. The earlier they are shown how to handle their anger and channel their aggressive impulses, the sooner the downward spiral can be halted.

The school suggested that whenever Marco was playing nicely that Sylvia make a big fuss of him. 'Praise the positive' became her motto.

Sylvia asked Marco if he would like to join a sports club. Marco jumped at the chance of going to the gym. He went twice a week and Sylvia found that he was much more relaxed on those evenings. They practiced some anger control techniques that had been suggested by the school. If Marco was feeling angry he was to count to ten while jumping up and down. Alternatively, he could take his special 'anger' cushion and yell at it or bash it.

Other children noticed the change in him, and soon Marco was inviting friends around to play. An 'upward spiral' had taken the place of the downward one. The safe haven he had wished for in his nightmare – the building to contain his angry feelings – had been established.

Dreamercises

reamercises are simple creative techniques I have devised to enable you to help your child enjoy dreaming and to derive the most benefit from their dreams. Using dreamercises also tends to increase self-confidence as your child develops their creativity and problem-solving skills.

This section contains eight dreamercises, each devised to meet a slightly different dreaming need. The first five encourage your child's creativity by providing ways in which they can choose what they dream about. Dreamercises 6, 7 and 8 are particularly good for dealing with nightmares and in opening communication with a child who is struggling with a problem in their life. As your confidence grows, you will want to devise your own dreamercises or create new variations on these tailored to suit your child in particular.

DREAMERCISE 1 – Happy Moments

This dreamercise provides your child with the opportunity to revisit and reflect on a funny incident or happy moment that is still alive in their memory, giving them rich material for their dreamlife. By sharing a treasured memory with you, your child may trigger memories of other happy moments in some way connected to the first but less consciously remembered by them.

When using this dreamercise you may be able to link a happy moment from real life with the subject of a recent dream as Will's mother did (*see page 46*).

As your child prepares for bed, ask them to recall a happy moment. Give them a framework: for example, 'from last summer'.

Ask them to recall it in as much detail as possible. Who was there? What time was it? Do they remember how they felt.

Now ask your child if they would like to relive this moment in their dreams. Suggest that they hold the memory of that happy moment at the forefront of their mind as they fall asleep.

DREAMERCISE 2 – Dream Replay

One of the simplest dreamercises, Dream Replay allows you to pick up on a pleasant dream your child has experienced and use it to promote in your child a contented state of mind, ready for further enjoyable dreams.

By using this dreamercise you demonstrate to your child that you have remembered a dream they have told you about and that you would like to hear them describe it again. This creates a closer bond between the two of you. Kiren's mother emphasized to her daughter how interested she was in her 'parade' dream when she suggested doing the Dream Replay dreamercise (*see page 45*). She took Dream Replay a step further by asking Kiren to complete her dream in a pleasant way of her choosing.

You could use Dream Replay during the day to provide ideas for a creative activity.

As your child gets ready for bed, ask them if they would like to 'replay' a lovely dream they have had: suggest a few recent happy dreams.

Once they have selected a dream, ask them to tell you the story of it again.

Give your child positive feedback with simple statements such as: 'I remember when you were so excited about that part!'

Ask them if they would like to replay their dream in their sleep.

Suggest they hold a happy image from the dream at the forefront of their mind as they slip into sleep. In this way your child may well replay the same positive dream that night.

DREAMERCISE 3 – Fairy-tale Ending

Frequently dreams do not finish with a 'tidy' ending: your child wakes up before the 'punch line'. Such dreams present you with the perfect opportunity for using the Fairy-tale Ending dreamercise. Children usually have a wealth of creative ideas and they love to have their imaginations stimulated. It is particularly good for your child's self-esteem to put them in control of creating a special storyline.

If your child recounts a dream to you that either did not 'finish' or lends itself to the creation of a fantastic ending, store the dream away in your mind until you have an evening with plenty of time to spend discussing possible endings with them. If, like Jane (*see page 74*), your child had an unfinished dream containing unpleasant feelings, follow her father's example and use the Fairy-tale Ending dreamercise to change the overriding 'bad' feeling by creating a wonderful ending. Try using a story as a springboard for the creation of some fantastic endings.

As your child gets ready for bed, ask them to recall a dream they have had without an ending or with an unsatisfactory ending. Then, as they are climbing into bed, ask them what fairy-tale ending they can create.

Encourage their craziest, most creative ideas. Be very positive in your praise for their ideas.

As they work through a new ending, ask them for details about all the aspects – characters, colours and events – to fill out the ending.

Once their fairy-tale ending is complete, further encourage your child by suggesting that their dream would now make a great story for creative writing or for drawing.

As they settle down to sleep, repeat to them the wonderful ending to their story and suggest that they can now visit their fairy-tale ending in dreamland.

DREAMERCISE 4 – Adventurous Journey

The essence of the Adventurous Journey dreamercise is to tap into your child's knowledge of the world and provide them with an exciting setting for a dream. It is great for stimulating conversation with your child and their interest in geography.

Your child has probably been made aware of a vast number of places around the world through his schoolwork, the movies, television, games and the Internet. Frequently, their knowledge of these places is scant and soon becomes lost among the wealth of detail n their minds. This dreamercise refocuses their mind on one or two of these places.

It is quite a creative enterprise to incorporate the world in general into a conversation about a particular dream your child would like to have. However, children delight in the challenge. For the quieter child, this dreamercise provides the opportunity to explore the 'world' through their imagination. By allowing them to be adventurous in their imagination, you help them to enjoy the smaller 'adventures' life has to offer.

At bedtime, ask your child where they would most like to visit in the world. Their response may amaze you.

Explore why they have chosen this place and what they think it would be like. Find the place in an atlas or reference book.

Encourage them to make up an adventurous journey to their chosen destination.

Suggest to them that they journey to that place in their dreams.

DREAMERCISE 5 – Dream Pathways

Dream Pathways is the perfect dreamercise for the slightly quieter, or shy child, who may also be quite artistic. It encourages your child to develop ideas, using both pictures and words, thus not only developing both individual abilities but linking the two creatively. The Dream Pathways dreamercise also provides your child with some fresh material to enrich their dreams.

If, like Samantha (*see page 102*), your child has encountered a problem or raised an issue of concern, suggest that they draw positive images relating to the matter. In this way, your child's Dream Pathway will become a way of negotiating what is troubling them or boosting their confidence over a particular issue.

This dreamercise can be done at any point during the day, and is ideal as the focus for a quiet time with your child in which they can wind down a little. You can then revisit their Dream Pathway at bedtime.

Ask your child to make a lively, creative drawing of three of four things they would like to see, visit or experience. Once their drawing is complete, discuss the images they have drawn.

Now ask your child to tell you a story connecting these images. For example, if they have drawn a rabbit, the Moon and an exotic plant, they may tell you that the rabbit is going to visit the Moon and on the Moon the rabbit will find exotic plants.

Ask your child to take a brightly coloured pencil and draw a pathway between the images, linking them in the way they have described. Call this their Dream Pathway.

At bedtime admire their drawing and talk about their Dream Pathway. Suggest that your child 'walk' down it in their dreams.

DREAMERCISE 6 – **Control Panel**

The Control Panel dreamercise gives your child the opportunity to talk about something that is bothering them and enables them to take control of a nightmare *(see Marco's and Andrew's experiences, pages 117 and 93)*, so that they will no longer be frightened of dreaming. If you wish, it can also be used purely as a creative drawing and dream-enhancing exercise.

This dreamercise can be adapted to suit a child of any age, whatever their needs. Choose a quiet moment when your child seems happy to open up a little with you to carry out this dreamercise: do not necessarily wait until bedtime.

Explore your child's nightmare in order to develop strategies for handling whatever is troubling them.

Give your child a large sheet of drawing paper and ask them to draw a control panel on it. Encourage them to use their imagination: the control panel can resemble that of any vehicle, from a spaceship to a car.

Ask your child to fill in masses of detail, and tailor it to suit their specific needs. For example, your child may be keen to include

on their panel a dump button to 'dump' unwanted nightmares, or an eject button to 'eject' any frightening thoughts. This is the opportunity for them to draw what will be most helpful to them.

Let your child take pride in their finished control panel. Pin it above their bed as Marco's mother did, so they can see it easily when they need a boost to their confidence.

At bedtime talk to your child about their control panel. Remind them they are now mistress or master of their dreams – they will not have a nightmare!

DREAMERCISE 7 – Bash the Baddy

The Bash the Baddy dreamercise is perfect when you feel strong action is needed to prevent the recurrence of a nightmare in your child. It is designed to increase your child's confidence after a frightening experience and to reassure them that you are on their side.

After establishing the root cause of the nightmare, try any of the techniques described below to help your child obliterate the nightmare images and overcome the problem. Jason's nightmare (*see page 82*) provides the perfect example of how this dreamercise can incorporate the root cause of the nightmare – the bullying – and the nightmare images themselves – the fearsome plants.

When your child is feeling secure and communicative, either during the day or at bedtime, try the Bash the Baddy dreamercise.

Ask your child to draw the nightmare image or to visualize it. If your child was 'frozen' in the nightmare like Alex (see page 110), try to incorporate as much action as possible.

Next you could ask your child to draw themselves as a very large giant and the nightmare image as tiny in comparison. They

can then, like Jason (see page 85), visualize what they as a giant would do to the tiny nightmare image. Alternatively, you could suggest that they tear up the picture of their nightmare image while repeating an affirmative statement such as: 'Now you can't frighten me, you're going in the garbage!' If your child is quite young, you could suggest that they hand you their nightmare drawing and as they do so say: 'My parent is going to take care of you! Good riddance!'

Tell your child confidently that they have the power to change frightening images into non-threatening ones. Advise them to 'bash the baddy' right out of their dream if the nightmare returns.

DREAMERCISE 8 – **Superhero**

The Superhero dreamercise is also designed primarily to prevent the recurrence of nightmares. Unlike the Bash the Baddy dreamercise, where nightmare images are disposed of in creative and active ways, the Superhero dreamercise allows your child to escape from involvement with the feared image by becoming a superhero.

Ask your child, if they could be any superhero what attributes would they choose to have. Would they be able to fly? Or perhaps they could disappear simply by saying some magic words. Let your child be as creative as they want to be.

Make a list of the attributes of your child's superhero. Then star the most important attribute on their list.

For younger children, suggest they draw a picture of themselves as the superhero. They can have fun with details, such as a mask.

Ask them to imagine that they are the superhero. Tell them that if their nightmare comes back they could put their special superhero attributes into operation. For example, if their star attribute is to be able to disappear, they could use this ability if the nightmare recurred, to avoid seeing the nightmare image. Encourage them to use more than one of their superhero attributes. For example, once they had disappeared, they might be able to fly away to their favorite place.

Reassure them that they can do these things in their dreams.

Your happy or fantastic dream

Your name:..

The name of your dream:...

....

Tell the story of your dream in words and pictures.

What were your favorite parts? What colors were in your dream? Were there any strange shapes? Were any of your friends or family in your dream?

Your unhappy dream or nightmare

Your name/superhero:...

Write the words or draw pictures of what makes you feel stronger and more powerful.

How will you fight the bad guys? Can you get away from them? Make up a happy ending to your dream in which you win.

Your positive or fantastic dream

Your name:...

The title of your dreamscape:...

....

Record your dreams here in words or pictures, or a combination of the two.

What were the dominant images in your dream? What do you think the hidden meaning of your dream was?

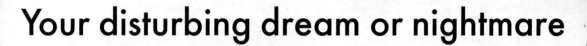

Your disturbing dream or nightmare

Your name:...

Record here in words or pictures, or a combination of the two, some ways in which you could take control of your nightmare.

How can you make the frightening images non-threatening? How can you make yourself feel more powerful? Can you create a place of safety or a way of escaping your nightmare? Can you change your nightmare so that it is no longer frightening?

Dream Directory

Individual images in your child's dream usually serve as the starting point for interpreting their dream. Remember, though, that both the context in which individual elements occur and the feelings experienced by the child when dreaming of them are crucial to understanding their meaning. For example, your child may dream of a lion entering their bedroom. In most cases, such an image would be threatening. However, if a sense of adventure permeated their dream and your child felt courageous rather than afraid, then the lion may represent recently conquered, or 'tamed', fears.

When analyzing your child's dream always bear in mind their age and relate the meanings given in this directory to your child's unique situation at home and at school. Talk to your child about their dream to gain a sense of how they felt about it overall. Or use the dream to sound them out about problems you were not aware of up to now. For example, your child may experience an unpleasant dream in which they are being rained on. If you are trying to train them to be dry at night they may feel over-pressurized and the rain might symbolize this pressure. Alternatively, if your child is older and you are anxious that they do well at school, the rain might symbolize this pressure.

There will always be dreams that seem indecipherable. Many children recall dreams that consist entirely of feelings and blurred or tangled images that they cannot be precise about. In such cases this directory is of only limited use but you can still discover a sense of what is happening in your child's emotional world from the feelings they describe. And talking about their dreams may lead to the development of a creative project or simply bring you closer together.

Animals, Birds and Insects

Pets: Family pets in children's dreams tend to represent security. Frequently, the dream consists of an adventure in which the pet is included. The child's subconscious may push the pet forward, particularly if they are feeling unsure of something (*see Zoe's dream, page 86*).

Animals: Horses are one of the most common dream symbols. They can represent a child's yearning for adventure. Your child may be ready for new activities if they dream of a galloping horse. Other animals may represent your child's natural curiosity (*see Gabriella's dream, page 62*).

Wild Animals: Lions and tigers are particularly common in younger children's dreams. Older children often dream of wolves, panthers, gorillas and other slightly more extraordinary wild animals. Frequently, these appear in nightmares. The appearance of wild animals in your child's dream may simply be the result of a recent visit to the zoo; on the other hand they may symbolize a particular fear. On exploration you may find that the wild animal represents a feared teacher or feared situation.

Birds: Birds frequently appear in the dreams of children who are yearning to move on. Very often the child literally flies away with the bird in the dream. In other dreams the bird arrives as if to deliver a message. Explore the emotions your child felt – was the bird's arrival accompanied by a sense of excitement, happiness or anxiety? Birds may also take on delightful qualities, reflecting your child's natural creativity (*see Jenny's dream, page 66*).

Insects: Insects in dreams often represent an irritation (*see Jane's dream, page 74*). They can assume frightening proportions in nightmares when a child may feel suffocated by their presence. If your child experiences such a nightmare try to discover what is overwhelming them during their waking life.

Exotic Animals, Birds and Insects: Sometimes images from the natural world take on incredible characteristics. This may be your child's subconscious having an 'artistic' field day (*see Stephie's dream, page 54*). If the symbols are nightmarish you may need to search deeper for an explanation (*see Chloe's dream, page 94*). If your child dreams of multi-legged creatures that reach out and trap them, they may feel unable to escape an unpleasant situation.

Buildings

Castles and Forts: A castle or fort can serve as a base for exploration and adventure *(see Will's dream, page 46)*. It can also be symbolic of a child's emotions or problems. The castle or fort may represent school or another situation your child is not coping with. If your child longs to scale the walls or break down the door, they feel excluded. If your child cannot escape a nightmarish castle or fort, they may feel isolated with a problem.

Churches: Often places of worship represent your child's awe at the natural world or their sense of the spiritual. If the image is frightening, your child may be haunted by too high expectations.

Houses: We expect images of houses to be comfortable for a child. If so, they feel confident within their family. Being lost in a house symbolizes anxiety within the home. Being locked out of the house indicates that your child feels excluded from the family – are siblings getting more attention?

Nondescript Buildings: Your child may describe a building that has no recognizable features. In this case the emotional content or the narrative of their dream needs consideration. Excitement or pleasure indicates a natural curiosity; fear or discomfort should be explored. The unfamiliarity coupled with feelings of being trapped, lost or locked out *(see above)* may mean that your child has a problem but cannot 'face' allowing the actual image to enter the dream. So, instead of their own home, school or friend's house, they remember a nondescript building *(see Andrew's dream, page 90)*.

Palaces: Ornate palaces indicate a creative nature. Not all children dream of such structures. Your child may be going through an imaginative phase that you can build on.

Costumes

Ornate Costumes: Ornate costumes may indicate a thoughtful and creative nature. The psychic energy involved in creating elaborate costumes symbolizes your child's development in this area. Sometimes it represents a child's ability to escape into the 'detail' of life.

Delight in Costume: Delight in wearing a costume, whatever its design, indicates a dramatic nature (*see Hanna's dream, page 22, Kiren's dream, page 42, and Jenny's dream, page 66*).

Dragged Down by Heavy Costume: Your child feels burdened, possibly by expectations that are too high.

Suffocated by Costume: This indicates that your child does not have enough freedom for emotional growth. They feel they cannot escape from the 'costume' imposed on them.

Shedding Costumes: This is analogous to a butterfly shedding its chrysalis. The child is ready for change or has outgrown or resolved a problem.

Familiar People

When familiar people feature in your child's dream it is important to check the emotions that accompany the image.

Parents: The changing nature of the parent/child relationship means that an unpleasant parent image may simply reflect a transitory problem, although it can indicate a longer-term difficulty.

Parent Looming: Your child feels a bit intimidated. Are you too strict or too harsh? Are you over-involved in their life? (*See Derek's dream, page 98.*)

Parent as Equal: This symbolizes contentment and confidence in the relationship your child has with you.

Tiny Parent or Parent Shrinks from Sight: Does your child feel they have too much responsibility, perhaps for you? Are you involving them in adult problems in the family?

Parent as a Shadow: The child feels emotionally abandoned. Have you been wrapped up too much in your own world? (*See Jane's dream, page 74; Chloe's dream, page 94; and Marco's dream, page 114.*)

Friends: Depending on your child's personality, their friendships may be up and down, stable or between the two. Their dreams may reflect the emotional nature of their close friendships.

Friends as Equals: This reveals your child's happiness with their friends.

Friends Hiding from your Child: Your child may feel isolated or lonely within their peer group.

Friends Taunting: Your child may be suffering from bullying or feel insecure with their friends (*see Andrew's dream, page 90 and Samantha's dream, page 102*).

Friends Following your Child: Either your child has assumed 'leadership' within a group, or would like to take a more active role (*see Kiren's dream, page 42*).

Relatives: Dreams that include relatives may give you an idea of your child's feelings about their extended family. This may be more or less important, depending on your circumstances. For example, if you have recently divorced you may wish your child to feel supported by the extended family. As with parents, a relative may loom large in a dream, appear as an equal (*see Steven's dream, page 58*), take a fun role, or shrink from sight.

Unusual or Unfamiliar People

Strangers in Nightmares: Sometimes a stranger who is frightening in a dream symbolizes a real person your child has difficulty with or is afraid of. Alternatively, the stranger may symbolize unpleasant feelings (*see Alex's dream, page 110*).

Strangers Asking Questions: This uncomfortable image may represent what is being asked of your child, at home or at school. Being under observation or questioned by strangers usually relates to anxiety of some sort.

Strangers Joining In: Your child may be lonely and adds new people to the events of their dreams to keep them company.

Pop Stars or Sports Stars: Your child may wish to emulate these modern 'role models'. They may aspire to achieve what the famous person has and create a fantastical dream where they are part of the pop group or sports team. Alternatively, they may find such people exciting and incorporate them in their dreams in an adventurous way.

Monarch, Leader of State, or other Official: Dreaming of such authoritative and traditional figures may have a variety of meanings, depending on their role:

Scolding: This may symbolize the authority of a teacher, and reflect your child's feelings towards that teacher.

Neutral: The presence of such an official may indicate that your child has reached a rather serious stage of their development or feelings.

Protective: If an authority figure is looking after your child, your child may need to feel protected. Does your child lack this in their relationship with you?

In Absurd Scenario: Their appearance in an absurd situation is probably the result of an active imagination that has included the figure because they were in the news.

Human Form

Admiring Self: This represents happiness with, and confidence in, themselves.

Being Naked: Your child may feel exposed or vulnerable. Is someone making them feel under attack?

Shedding Body Parts: Your child may be fearful of something and is trying to shed that fear, which is symbolized by an arm or a leg. A body part can be shed and alter its appearance (*see Samantha's dream, page 102*).

Frozen Body: If your child was frozen by fear, or could not move in their dream, they are experiencing emotional upset which they are unable to cope with.

Finding a Body Part: This may symbolize solving a problem. Your child literally picks up the pieces and puts them together like a puzzle.

Landscapes

Rivers: A fast-flowing river tends to mean that things are moving too fast for your child. The rushing water is usually quite threatening. They may feel they are being carried away or that something is beyond their control. If the river is calm and flowing gently it may symbolize a natural curiosity – where does it lead?

Lakes: Floating in a lake, either unaided or in a boat, symbolizes calmness. Children usually feel their emotions are 'contained' in such dreams.

Oceans/Seas: Calm, non-threatening seas can symbolize a determination to meet a challenge (*see Sam's dream, page 38*). Fearsome swells or being battered in a boat would be nightmarish and symbolize out-of-control emotions.

Dense Forests: These are foreboding and symbolize the unknown. Such a forest may relate to uncomfortable emotions experienced by your child, or worry about something, perhaps an exam.

Lush Forests: These may symbolize a period of intellectual or emotional growth in your child. The wonder and mystique of such an image reflects their developing interest in life (*see Gabriella's dream, page 62*).

Parks/Parkland: Usually indicate that your child is enjoying life. Open parkland full of pleasant images reflects a positive sense of wellbeing and perhaps playfulness, depending on the detail.

Empty Landscapes: If accompanied by unpleasant emotions, a barren landscape usually means your child feels lonely or isolated (*see Jack's dream, page 70*).

Fantastical Landscapes: Wildly exciting landscapes demonstrate the innate creativity of your child (*see Stephie's dream, page 54*).

Natural Phenomena

Fire: Fire can represent primitive, undeveloped emotions – the ferocity, the flames and the smoke are all frightening. If nothing is containing the fire in your child's dream, they may have some very strong emotions that they feel are out of control. Sometimes children 'play' with fire in their dreams. This may be a reference to the lessons parents have been teaching during waking hours or can symbolize a playful nature.

Rain: If your child dreams of a harsh, driving storm they may feel 'battered' in their waking life by something. Perhaps someone is being very strict with them.

Rainbows: A beautiful rainbow usually symbolizes the happiness your child feels with life at that moment. It can also inspire hours of pleasure through artwork (*see Stephie's dream, page 54*).

Wind: A fierce, strong wind may symbolize your child's sense that they are fighting something. If they are being buffeted they may feel they lack control over a particular aspect of their life.

Realistic Places with Unusual Qualities

Children often elaborate commonplace features in their dreams. For example, their home acquires the proportions of a palace or their garden is endowed with secret passages and mysterious plants. Frequently, these amazing qualities provide exceptional enjoyment (*see Steven's dream, page 58*).

When such dream imagery takes on unpleasant or nightmarish qualities the child's subconscious may be making an attempt to camouflage unpleasant thoughts or feelings related to the real place. The unrealistic features of the images serve as a distraction.

Unusual Phenomena

Flying without Fear: If your child soared with delight then they feel carefree and happy with their present circumstances. They are literally flying through life.

Flying with Fear: If your child reports anxiety or fear in a dream about flying they may feel unsupported in some aspect of their life. If, for example, they were fearfully flying above their school something may be upsetting them there.

Swooping: Flying about like a magical

fairy in a dream, swooping through the air and delighting in the sensation, symbolizes a great sense of playfulness in your child.

Very Tall: If your child finds themselves to be very tall in a dream, they may feel out of place. Somehow your child feels they have unwanted attention or do not fit in. If this occurs in a fantastical dream where everything has taken on unusual proportions it may simply reflect their imagination.

Very Small: If your child dreams of being very small they may feel insignificant. Do they need more recognition or attention? If part of a fantastical dream, it may simply reflect their imagination.

Shapes that Change: When a shape or an object suddenly transforms into something else, it may be playful – a reflection of your child's natural creativity – or nightmarish. In Samantha's dream (*see page 102*), the changing face on the doll is threatening and in Jason's dream (*see page 82*), when the gate grows taller to

make escape impossible, it is terrifying. The changing form may represent what is troubling the child: it may start as an innocent shape but as the real image bursts through, it becomes frightening.

Negative, Disturbing or Strange Feelings

Your child may tell you that they have had a dream but when questioned they can tell you nothing of what has actually happened in the dream. Often younger children experience feelings they cannot label, while children of all ages sometimes find it hard to describe and discuss problems with their parents. In their dreams these feelings or problems may be experienced as emotion without accompanying images.

Adriana's dream (*see page 78*) provides a similar example to this: she describes a sense of being trapped in what she guesses to be a rolling ball. If your child describes a feeling or 'sense' to you without being able to give you any details, discuss the feelings they recall, and ask them if they are reminded of any feelings they have experienced during waking hours. This may give you clues as to what has caused the discomfort that has then been transferred to their dream.

School Themes

Empty School: This represents a sense of being left behind. Does your child feel left behind academically or socially.

Dilapidated School: If your child dreams of a crumbling, dilapidated school building, they may feel there is not much there for them. Perhaps they have not enjoyed school and cannot understand its value. They need your encouragement to find out how school life may benefit them.

Bright, Attractive School: If your child's school image is a positive, they do not feel threatened by being at school. Keep on encouraging them.

Faceless Teachers: Removing the face of a person in a dream is symbolic of having 'nothing in common' with that person. Quite literally, you do not want to know them. Your child is rejecting their teacher perhaps because they feel their teacher is rejecting them.

Teacher Ignores your Child: If your child feels ignored by a teacher, try to discover if they feel insignificant in class. They may need encouragement to speak up more in class discussions so the teacher notices them in a positive way. If the image is accompanied by very negative feelings, you may need to explore how the teacher is treating your child.

Teacher with Unusual Features: For the appearance of very tall or very small teachers, please refer to the relevant entries in Unusual Phenomena (*see page 136*). Unusual features in a teacher may reveal a lot about your child's relationship with that teacher. Try to discover the accompanying feelings your child had and the particular situation.

Positive Teacher: If your child recounts a happy or positive image of their teacher their relationship is probably very good.

Teacher Mistreats Child: Unhappiness with a teacher may take the form of an unusual method of mistreatment. Tiffany was made fun of by her teacher in her dream, demonstrating her feelings of being undermined by that teacher (*see page 106*). Mistreatment may take many forms and it is important to explore what it could mean to your child.

Being Embarrassed in class: Dreaming of embarrassment in class may symbolize some sort of humiliating experience your child has had during lessons. Could they have been ridiculed by their teacher? Perhaps they were late with schoolwork.

Front of the Class: Finding themselves at the front of the class is a common symbol of anxiety. The child is 'on show' and feels under scrutiny. If accompanied by positive feelings your child feels secure within the classroom setting.

Different Things Happening in Class: Classroom dreams often contain events unrelated to teaching. The child is so familiar with the classroom that they play out other themes using the classroom as a backdrop. If it has been used as a 'stage' for a completely unrelated 'play' look at the content of the dream: the meaning will be held in the action rather than the setting.

Enjoyment in the Playground: Many children find the experience of playground socialization unsettling. It is in the playground that the pecking order gets established and groups form, and children frequently have anxiety-filled dreams set there. So a positive playground dream symbolizes your child's adjustment to these challenges.

Intimidation in the Playground: Does the playground take on nightmarish qualities? Is your child distressed by the dream? You may need to help them with coping strategies to get on with others in the playground environment.

Fantastic Playground: An exciting or fantastical playground is a sign of your

child's great enjoyment. They are thriving in the playground environment.

School Children: Your child may dream of their peer group at school in the same way as they dream about their friends (*see Familiar People, page 132*). However, a dream in which your child feels taunted by their friends may hold a deeper meaning than a dream in which they are taunted by some children unknown to them. Bear in mind the importance of the relationship and how keenly your child may feel negative situations.

School Children with Unusual Features: As with dreams featuring any unusual phenomena (*see page 136*), explore the accompanying emotion your child felt in their dream. This may indicate whether your child is simply being creative or whether their subconscious is trying to protect them from feelings of anxiety regarding their peer group at school.

Toys

Magical Toys: Toys that 'come to life' in dreams symbolize the wishful thinking of younger children and the creativity of older ones. If the dream is accompanied by feelings of loneliness, it may mean your child is trying to create a 'friend' through the toy. If a toy coming to life takes on nightmarish proportions, it may symbolize a problem your child is experiencing – the unconscious veils the problem by use of a toy. The toy may represent a person your child is troubled by *(see Samantha's dream, page 102).*

Familiar Toys: Children often incorporate their favorite possessions into their dreamscapes. Children become very attached to particular toys, so it is not surprising that they feature in their dreams. You may even find they include objects like treasured blankets or other personal items. Having an adventurous

dream accompanied by a favourite toy provides the child with a sense of security.

Transportation

Children's dreams are full of symbols concerning transportation. This is hardly surprising as their lives and personalities change so rapidly, and transportation very often symbolizes a time to move forward. It is important to explore the feelings attached to the symbols as the meaning can vary a great deal.

Airplanes: Flying a plane can represent taking charge of a situation. The responsibility and glamour of being a 'pilot' 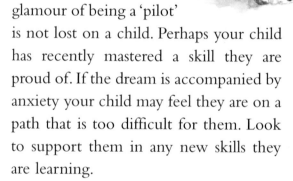 is not lost on a child. Perhaps your child has recently mastered a skill they are proud of. If the dream is accompanied by anxiety your child may feel they are on a path that is too difficult for them. Look to support them in any new skills they are learning.

Racing Cars: If your child dreams of racing about in a speeding car they may simply be fulfilling a wish for the sort of excitement children adore. It may also symbolize the speed with which they are meeting the ever-growing demands on them. If being in a racing car is frightening, then it may symbolize their feelings careering out of control.

Family Cars: A dream set in a family car usually demonstrates settled, contented feelings about family life. If accompanied by fear or anxiety your child may feel trapped by a problem within the family that they have not been able to solve.

Rockets/Spaceships: Soaring through space usually occurs in fantastical dreams like Antonio's (*see page 50*). Children are amazed by images of outer space and will incorporate these into their dreams. If space themes occur in nightmares they may represent fears your child has not wanted to face. Camouflaged in this way, they are protected from having to face the real issue of concern.

Trains: Trains symbolize persistence: as the train chugs along, so does your child.

Trucks: A big, chunky truck symbolizes a strong will. If your child describes driving along in such a vehicle you can be sure their confidence is high. If a truck careers out of control it may represent your child's feelings that they have too heavy a load to carry.

Unusual Modes: The child who dreams up their own unusual transportation is at a creative point. This may reflect a need to do things differently. Encourage their unique ways of getting on with tasks. If accompanied by fear or a feeling of being out of control, the unusual symbolism may mask a problem they are trying to cope with.

Walls, Fences and other Structures

Scaling Walls: If unaccompanied by anxiety then it may represent your child's aspiration to do their best.

Not Being Able to See Over: This symbolizes a sense of frustration. What cannot your child do right now? Do they feel held back in some way?

Fences and Gates: These can be protective or exclusive, a structure to climb over or under or to peer through – see page 37 for detailed examples. (*See Sophie's dream, page 35, and Jason's dream, page 82.*)

Climbing on Structures: If the structure does not take a particular shape it usually represents an adventurous stage in which anything seems possible.

Hanging from Structures: Your child may need more parental support than they are receiving. If they feel they are about to drop, then they may have been struggling with something for a while.

Index

Author's Acknowledgements

I enjoyed writing *Understanding Your Child's Dreams* tremendously. This enjoyment was made possible by the help I received from many people and through the conversations I've had with parents over a number of years. Their generosity of time, honesty about their children and their dreams, and enthusiasm for looking at their children's emotional life in a new way, were of enormous value. I'd also like to thank friends and family for putting up with the 'bunker mentality' approach I adopted when I was writing. Their patience and wisdom allowed them to know that one day my life would be back to normal and I would be worth knowing again. Special thanks go to Liz Wheeler who has not only become a friend but is a wonderful editor, and Jane Laing who truly understood what I was trying to convey in this book. Marissa Feind and Caroline Uff have ensured that the design and beautiful illustrations represented the creativity, emotionality and interpretation of the dreams in a clear fashion.

A final thank you goes to children everywhere, their natural optimism, emotional openness and innate creativity, that we as adults may learn from.

EDDISON • SADD EDITIONS

Commissioning Editor: Liz Wheeler
Project Editor: Jane Laing
Proofreader: Sarah Larter
Art Director: Elaine Partington
Senior Designer: Marissa Feind
Production: Karyn Claridge, Charles James